GOD SAID YES!

from tragedy to triumph

ENDORSEMENTS

Marolyn's healing miracles are profound. So is her life faithfully lived out as a beloved daughter of God. Throughout her incredible, well-recorded miracle journey, Marolyn chose to believe that life's circumstances do not change the reality of God's goodness. The agony of waiting that is sometimes involved in our process for a miracle is recorded carefully and honorably. Hope springs from these pages. *God Said Yes! Triumph Over Tragedy* has deeply impacted me. I encourage everyone who is on a journey pressing in for a miracle to read this book.

—**Bill Johnson**, Bethel Church, Redding, CA, author of *When Heaven Invades Earth* & *God is Good*

Marolyn Ford, a blind woman who sees, a woman who can't eat or drink but lives, is able to summon hope from any hopeless situation. Her source of hope is infinite.

—**David Waters**, journalist, The Commercial Appeal of Memphis

The God of miracles lives and is active today. His supernatural presence and gifts are as real today as in the first century. I heard Marolyn Ford's testimony in person, and I have seen what God is still doing today. Her story will thrill you as you read the witness of one who was 'once blind' but 'now sees.'

—**Ron Phillips,** Abba's House, Chattanooga, TN

Having been a witness to my wife's recovery after a serious illness, I have no doubt God is in the healing business. Whether physically or spiritually, He is sovereign and knows our every need. I pray this book will be an inspiration and a reminder to lean on Him.

—Dr. Ed Wheat, World-renown marriage counselor and Best-selling Author

GOD SAID YES!

from tragedy to triumph

DR. MAROLYN FORD

PUBLISHING THE POSITIVE

ELK LAKE PUBLISHING INC
Plymouth, Massachusetts

Cover and Interior Design: Derinda Babcock

Editor(s): Cheryl Ricker, Max Dixon, Jeanne Marie Leach, Deb Haggerty

Author Represented by: Cheryl Ricker

PUBLISHED BY: Elk Lake Publishing, Inc., 35 Dogwood Dr., Plymouth, MA 02360, 2019

Library Cataloging Data

Names: [Ford, Marolyn] (Marolyn Ford)

God Said Yes! From Tragedy to Triumph / Marolyn Ford

228 p. 23cm × 15cm (9in × 6 in.)

Description: Dr. Marolyn ford has experienced miraculous healings not once, but twice in her life—all through the power of prayer.

Identifiers: ISBN-13: 978-1-951080-11-2 (trade) | 978-1-951080-12-9 (POD) | 978-1-95108013-6 (e-book) | 978-1-951080-14-3 (trade hardcover)

Key Words: blindness, miracles, prayer, memoir, digestive paralysis, inspirational, marriage

LCCN: 2019945615 Nonfiction

DEDICATION

For Acie,

You loved me unconditionally throughout our fifty-two years of marriage. A husband dedicated to our wedding vows of "till death we part," you trusted in God's faithfulness no matter how dark the path. Time and again, you were my steady rock to lean on. Though our earthly partnership has ended, an appreciation of your love for your Creator and for me lingers on. God's servant with a humble spirit, you were truly a gift to me. I miss you, Acie, and will always love you.

—Marolyn

Lord, help me to

Live today, what I will

One day have wished

I had in eternity.

—Author unknown

TABLE OF CONTENTS

PART I
Miracle I

1

Shattered Dreams

"Why are you calling me up here to do your work?" Gertrude asked in frustration. "I have my own work to do."

I'd been sitting at my desk, stuffing billing statements into envelopes for about twenty or thirty minutes after my vision became blurry. At first, I thought some sort of film was covering my eyes, but after much blinking and rubbing, the blurriness didn't change. I had to prepare the billing invoices once a month, so I continued on with my work, but the aggravation in my eyes didn't get any better.

Trembling, I finally said, "I don't know what's wrong. I can't see clearly. Everything is a blur." I'd only recently graduated from E.E. Fell Holland High School and taken this office job a few weeks prior. This wasn't normal. I was having serious difficulty, not just an aggravation.

"What do you mean you can't see?" Gertrude asked.

"Everything's all blurry, Gert," I said, trying to stay calm and keep my composure. "Even you look blurred." I fought back the tears welling up within me out of fear, hoping no one would notice. I was scared and wanted to get out of there. I stood to my feet, unsteady.

"Can you see Annie?" Gertrude asked. "She's standing about fifteen feet from you."

I squinted to bring my eyes into focus but to no avail. "No, I can't see her." The office with all its pictures, books, plants, doorways, and people had become one huge mesh of blended color. What was happening to me?

My heart pounded, and I now trembled uncontrollably.

Gertrude phoned an ophthalmologist in a panic. "One of our workers can't see. She was fine one minute, and then everything suddenly went blurry." She hung up and announced that the doctor wanted me to come in right away.

I was thankful for her quick action.

"One of us will go with you," she said.

Call it stubborn or whatever you want, but I wanted to get away from people. I needed to be alone, not with someone in the car asking questions. I grabbed my things and headed out the door, shaking but determined.

Only one thing was clear to me—I could barely see enough to do this. I could make out the bleary sidewalk and walked the couple of blocks to the ophthalmologist's office.

I finally entered the doctor's office feeling strange and out of sorts. The receptionist guided me to the exam room with charts on the walls.

When a doctor came in to test me, I couldn't even see the big "E" at the top of the chart. I struggled to think positively. Surely, he'd give me some kind of medication, and this would all clear up.

"Do I have an infection?" I asked.

"It doesn't appear so."

My heart pounded in my chest.

The doctor had been bending over as he looked into my eyes. He stood up, took in a deep breath, and let out a sigh. "Marolyn, I really don't know what caused this abrupt visual loss," he declared.

I squeezed my hands together as I tried to see his blurry face. I would've asked questions, but I was too afraid of his answers. Our visit concluded with the doctor giving me medication and telling me to return to see him the following day. I was thankful he wanted to see me again that soon.

After leaving his office, I still wanted to be alone and didn't want to talk to anyone. I'd have to wait until my mother got off work to catch a ride home. I needed time to think. If I walked back toward my place of work, I'd arrive there just before she'd be coming by to pick me up. I still held hope this blurriness would clear up overnight and wear off. So, I decided not to mention it to my mom. I didn't need to worry her too. Whether it cleared up or not, I was buying time before saying something to her about it. I figured I had enough vision that I could recognize the car when she drove up.

I walked back to the cycle shop, praying under my breath until she arrived. I barely recognized our car.

"Keys?" she said, handing them to me like she usually did.

I shook my head. "No thanks."

"What, you don't want to drive?"

"Ah, I'm not feeling very well."

"Oh, okay."

My guess is she thought I was tired.

When we got home, I asked to be excused from helping with the meal and hurried to my room. Every movement was an awkward stumble, and I had to feel for the stairs with the tips of my toes. I stayed in my room that evening to be alone. I was young. Surely, the fuzziness would only be temporary. Something like this didn't happen to young people. I was too scared to put it into words and talk about it, so I stayed in my room and prayed.

"God, may this medication clear everything up." I lay on my bed and pulled the covers over my head. "And God ... when morning comes, please may everything return back to normal."

I didn't sleep much that night.

Early the next morning in my first waking moments, everything was fine until I opened my eyes. No, it couldn't be! Everything was blurry again but worse.

I stared at the hazy ceiling, wishing away this nightmare. Tears burned behind my eyes as I dragged myself out of bed and fumbled to get ready for work. Yes, I actually went back to work. I didn't want to lose my office job, so I dressed. My mom always said, *if there's a will, there's a way. Get out there and figure it out.*

I grew up in a household where we didn't make excuses not to go to work. I figured stuffing envelopes was one thing I could find a way to do without good vision, and maybe my vision would improve throughout the day.

Having been born a natural blonde, I always put on my makeup, even if I wasn't going anywhere. Without makeup, we blonde-headed girls have no color in our eyebrows or lashes; therefore, makeup was a must for me. I worked at it that day and every day thereafter.

I had to feel around for my eyebrows to touch them up with the pencil. That's when I realized I couldn't distinguish dark and light shades of makeup. Did I look like a clown or what? Maybe people wouldn't look too closely.

At work, the only thing I could do was stuff monthly statements into envelopes. Thankfully, it was billing time, so I needed to do that anyway. However, like yesterday, I needed extra help when people came in to pay their bills. I had to call someone from the back to come write out a receipt for me, which didn't exactly help my coworkers' frustration levels.

That afternoon at my doctor's appointment, I shook so much I had to wrap my arms around my body to calm down. I was so nervous even my insides were shaking. How I wanted to hear an encouraging word.

First, the doctor asked if I could see anything on the chart in front of me.

"No," I answered. "Nothing."

When the doctor looked into my eyes, I expected at least a sliver of encouraging news. "I'm sorry, Marolyn," he said in a grim tone of voice, "but nothing has changed."

"Nothing?" I couldn't believe what I heard. There had to be something that could be done. Nervously, I asked, fear dripping from every word, "What am I going to do?"

"Now, we send you to the Holland Hospital for testing."

That thought frightened me. I'd never been inside the hospital before. The time came for me to tell Mom why I hadn't driven the car or helped with the work around the house for a couple days. My stomach churned. How could I tell her what was going on when I didn't really know myself? The doctor didn't have any idea either.

My excitement about going to college was suddenly replaced by a heavy weight of dread and uncertainty.

Instead of helping cook that night, I excused myself and sat in Dad's chair by the record player in the living room, listening to God's music. Minutes slipped into hours.

Mom came in with crossed arms, cleared her throat, and asked, "Are you ok? What exactly is going on?"

"Well, I don't really know," I answered. "I hadn't been feeling well. The fact is, I've been having a hard time seeing. I didn't want to say anything or worry you with it. I thought it would clear up in a day or two. Everything just went blurry while at work. All I can see are outlines of things. I can't even see your face."

"My word, girl! We've got to get you to the doctor!"

"I already went, and he doesn't know what's wrong with me."

"You went to the doctor, and he doesn't know what's wrong?"

"He gave me some medicine, and I've already been taking that."

"We'll, give it a day or two. I'm sure it'll clear up," she said.

"It's already been nearly two days and nothing's changed."

"Well, it has to clear up." Her voice softened. "It just has to."

We were a family that never thought the worst or jumped to a bad conclusion before all the facts were in, so we left it at that.

I was so scared at that moment; I didn't want her to voice anything more than that. I fought hard to keep that same attitude. *Surely, Mom's right. This will clear up.*

Mom drove me to my appointment at the hospital. When the test all came back clear—which was good but still not an answer—I was heartbroken and discouraged. I wanted a quick fix.

My doctor then arranged for me to see the doctors at the Ann Arbor Michigan Medical Center for Eyes. That perked me up. It sounded good to me. New hope sprang up within me.

As much as I didn't want to lose my job, I resigned my secretarial position.

All the testing done at the Ann Arbor Medical center proved nothing either. Discouraged, I thought I'd run out of options; however, when I returned to see my home doctor, he sent me to the specialists at the Mayo Clinic in Rochester, Minnesota. This was another option. New hope sprang up in me. Over three days at Mayo, I was pricked, prodded, and x-rayed some more. They were our last hope. These medical doctors are the top of the line in medicine. They'd have all the answers I was looking for, and they'd have a positive outcome for me.

The Mayo doctor gave Mom and me their final diagnosis. "Marolyn has severe Juvenile Macular Degeneration," the doctor said, "a hereditary loss of central vision. Holes and scar tissue have developed in each eye, resulting in dead nerve endings. The damage in both eyes is permanent." His voice sounded cold as he recounted this to Mom. Then he turned to me. "Marolyn, that means you're legally blind. There's nothing we can do to correct that. No surgery, medication, or glasses. I suggest you go home and learn to live with it."

No! No! I can't! You have to be able to do something! My stomach knotted as fear of the unknown overwhelmed me.

I felt sick, and my joints went weak. I was glad I was still sitting in a chair, or I would have crumpled to the floor from hearing his words.

Permanent? Nothing they can do? How? There has to be some kind of mistake. This couldn't be true. I was only eighteen and had my whole life ahead of me—college, career, marriage. How could blindness be my new reality?

Mom asked a few questions of the doctor. I was so devastated I couldn't say a word. Heartbroken, we both walked out of the Mayo clinic in silence. Crushed beneath the load, neither of us could speak about it on the drive home. I cried the entire way.

I didn't know the eight-hour drive home could be so heavy. I'd been bursting with dreams and the rush of excitement that comes after graduating and transitioning into adulthood. With the doctor's words, those dreams had shattered into unanswerable questions.

I couldn't read or write, so how could I go to college? How could I get married? Who would want to date, and then marry a blind girl? How could I make a living and care for myself? Would I have to be dependent on others? That terrifying thought made my bones creep.

How could I go on without being able to see a bird, a leaf, a sentence in a book, or a smile on someone's face? I tried to swallow the lump in my chest. These thoughts were more than I could bear to think about. This was weighty. *Oh God, how do I go on? Why? This is more than I can handle.* I wanted to be alone to cry and scream, to grieve in my own solitary place. I'd gone down in despair and couldn't go any lower. I'd only wanted something … some glimmer of hope, but they gave me none.

Only a few days ago, I'd gazed across our farm's flatlands at the crops waving in the wind and at the soothing green trees beneath an opulent blue sky with very blurred vision. Tears welled up in my eyes. Would I never be able to see the change of seasons again? Harvest, with its explosion of reds, oranges, and yellows, was my favorite time of the year. The beauty of winter with the sun's rays shimmering through icicles from rooftops and trees. Would I never be able to watch them glisten against the carpet of freshly fallen snow? Nature had always filled my heart with calmness as I marveled at God's handiwork. What now?

The continual space of silence between my mom and me bothered me as I pressed my face against the car's cool window and stared into the blurry distance. *God, aren't you in control anymore?*

Nebulous images zipped by as miles turned into hours. Mom wasn't familiar with expressway driving. She had to keep her mind on her driving as we left the big city of Rochester, Minnesota. I craved a warm hand on my shoulder and a tender word of encouragement, but nothing came.

GOD SAID YES!

My mother was a wonderful mom, but she, too, was drowning in a sea of her own grief, and she didn't know how to respond to my suffering that day. She probably thought I needed space. I couldn't see her face but sensed her worry and helplessness. She normally conversed easily, but when I needed her most, I didn't have her for support and encouragement. Instead, during this heartbreaking time, we rode together but separately, and I descended into a pit, empty and alone.

2

COULD I BELIEVE?

Nothing prepared me for the shift from a seeing world to a sightless one. Nothing. Having grown up on a sprawling farm made it even more difficult. We were a family of nine, which meant plenty of chores for all. I'm convinced our parents planted the seed of hard work in us from the moment we popped out of the womb, and by the time we were walking, that seed had grown into a well-rooted tree.

One of my first serious assignments was gathering eggs from a thousand or more chickens. And, about the age of seven, we three girls started hoeing acre-long rows in the garden and gathered fruit and vegetables, which we either canned or put in the freezer. Meanwhile, Dad and our four brothers milked cows and tended to more physical chores like plowing, dragging, and disking the ground before planting and harvesting.

By the time I turned nine, my twin, Carolyn, and I drove the straight transmission flatbed truck and John Deere tractor and trailer from one hay bale to another across the fields while the boys loaded it up with either hay bales or wheat, sometimes both. We also cooked family meals when Mom was busy and helped her with dishwashing, housecleaning, baking, laundry, and ironing.

As I grew into my teens, I loved working in the fields, cultivating corn, and bringing in the harvest.

One by one, the boys married and found work in the city to support their families. We girls had to pitch in to fill the gaps, but we knew little about repairing the equipment when it broke down in the field. The boys had always tended to that.

Now, not only was I blind and fumbling around, but guilt bore into me because I could no longer contribute to our family's strong work ethic and team mentality. Instead of being an asset, I'd become a burden with a dwindling sense of self-worth.

In the months ahead, I could no longer hold a paying job. To make matters worse, my twin and confidant, Carolyn, started attending college in Tennessee. She was moving on with her life while I was stuck back at home.

"God!" I cried out. "How do I do this? How do I live with this blindness?"

No answer came. The silence grew like a dark, hollow chamber. Yet, somehow deep down, I knew God was with me. He wouldn't leave me alone. He promised in his Word that he would never leave me or forsake me and that he would remain faithful. Could I believe it?

On Sunday evening, people arrived at church thirty minutes before the service began. This wasn't uncommon as we would use this preservice time to pray and read our Bibles while the organist played. For the Sunday morning service, we sat together as a family, but for the evening services, we young people sat in the balcony. I was sixteen at the time and decided I would read verses on prayer I found listed in my concordance.

"Delight yourself in the LORD; and He will give you the desires of your heart" (Psalm 37:4).

"If you abide in Me, and My words abide in you, ask whatever you wish, and it will be done for you." (John 15:7).

"Therefore I say to you, all things for which you pray and ask, believe that you have received them, and they will be *granted* you." (Mark 11:24).

"And without faith it is impossible to please *Him*, for he who comes to God must believe that He is and *that* He is a rewarder of those who seek him" (Hebrews 11:6).

These promises were so wonderful! God said I could ask anything whatsoever, according to his will, and it would be done. And he is "able to do far more abundantly beyond all that we ask or think, according to the power that works within us" (Ephesians 3:20). These verses gripped me as the promises exploded in my heart and flooded my soul with joy. God couldn't have made his word clearer to me that evening as I sat in the balcony surrounded by my friends. Truly the entrance of his Word had brought light to my heart.

Then I asked God why people didn't believe his Word exactly as he gave it. He said he'd do all these wonderful things above all we can ask or think?

After this infusion of faith, Satan came to me, saying, "People don't actually take these verses literally." Doubts came rolling in like a flood over my spirit. Rather than taking a firm stand, I allowed the devil to snatch the truth of what I had just read from me.

In spite of that 'test of faith' incident, my faith in God was established while I was still young, and I grew in faith as I've hidden his Word in my heart. This foundation sustained through the challenges I faced later in life.

Back when I could see, I used to venture to several special places on the farm to talk to God. These areas had been havens of prayer because his presence seemed especially near. I could gaze out for miles across the Michigan flatlands at the crops blowing in the wind before the harvest. Now, I could no longer see the picturesque meadow or feel the peace it brought to my soul. Instead, I felt a heavy, gray haze and a deep sense of sadness.

With limited mobility, I only had one place outside where I could commune with God and feel safe—under the shade of our huge one-hundred-year-old maple tree my grandfather planted. The giant tree proudly stood in the one-acre front yard between our house and the driveway. I could find the old maple by walking alongside the house and staying on the patch of grass between the driveway and the house.

Our sixty acres surrounding the house connected to miles of farmland. The closest neighbor was about a half mile away. The other neighbor lived a mile up the road with nothing but farmland between us.

During those first weeks, I sat beneath the tree's protective branches and ran my hands through the soft grass. Cool wind danced across my face as the summer sun's heat diminished in strength, and I breathed sweet aromas of dirt and flowers. With my sight gone, smell and touch became more pronounced and precious. There under that old tree, I told God my deepest, most painful feelings. I always felt I could be honest with him. Not disrespectful, but honest, even when angry. I was his child, so he could handle it.

I'd always asked God to take my life and use it for his purposes. As a child, I knew he was listening and visiting with me. But how could he take my life and use it for good now?

Why did you let this happen, God? Do You really care? Where are you?

3

BREAKTHROUGH

Upon returning home from Mayo Clinic, the sadness could be so overwhelming at times I couldn't even go to the old maple tree. I couldn't pray or do anything. All I could do was sit in Dad's easy chair and listen to gospel records. I needed that time to grieve over the life I had lost. The song sung by Ethel Walters in the Billy Graham Crusades, "His Eye Is On The Sparrow" by Charles H. Gabriel filled the room. The lyrics went like this:

> Whenever I am tempted, whenever clouds arise,
> When songs give place to sighing, when hope within me dies,
> I draw the closer to Him, from care He sets me free;
> His eye is on the sparrow, and I know He watches me;
> His eye is on the sparrow, and I know He watches me.
>
> I sing because I'm happy,
> I sing because I'm free,
> For His eye is on the sparrow,
> And I know He watches me.

I sat there listening to the song over and over, trying to find comfort by letting the music and words wash over my fears and my soul.

"Oh God," I finally cried, almost in a whisper. "You care so much for those little birds that fly. You feather them and feed them. If one sparrow falls to the ground, you know. Lord, if you care that much about the little birds, surely, you'll take care of me. I'm your child."

While sitting in Dad's chair day after day, I encountered many moments of reflection like that. Could God *really* take care of me? Could I trust him? Frequently, I reminded God of his Word by quoting Scripture promises back to him.

"Trust in the LORD with all your heart And do not lean on your own understanding. In all your ways acknowledge Him, and He make your paths straight" (Proverbs 3:5-6).

And in Matthew 6:25-26, God says, "Do not be worried about your life … Look at the birds of the air … your heavenly Father feeds them. Are you not worth much more than they?" I held on to anything I could to find strength to cope.

Listening to the records and considering how God cares for the birds anchored me during those dark hours.

I listened to Jack Holcomb sing the song, "Until Then." The words tell us our hearts should sing until God calls us home. The words convicted me because my heart wasn't singing. I was mumbling the words, but they weren't planted in my spirit. I was still crying every day. One cannot sing and cry at the same time. I realized I had to make a choice. Would I sing and praise him through the tears, even when I didn't feel like it?

That's when I realized I wouldn't get my needed breakthrough by singing quietly to myself.

I'm sure the apostle Paul and Silas didn't feel like singing as they sat on that cold, damp, hard floor in the jail with their wrists and ankles bleeding from chains. Still, they lifted their voices to praise God. And while they sang, his power came down, their chains fell off, the prison doors flung open, and they were suddenly free. Could that happen to me?

Somewhere during those weeks of reflection and listening to the music, I came to ponder life, even with its hardships, as a gift. Could God use this blindness—this affliction from the evil one—in a special way? If so, what would I do with that gift if it were up to me? Whether I was blind or could see, I had only one life to live, and I wanted to be able to stand before Jesus knowing I lived a life of faithfulness. After all, he died on the cross for me. Anything I could offer back to him was a gift.

Sitting in a pool of sadness the rest of my life wouldn't exactly be the best gift to give him. Even though I still cried and grieved over the life I'd lost, somehow, I needed to pick up the broken pieces and pull my life together. I needed to get alone with God—really alone—and cry out to him like never before. And this time Dad's chair and the old maple tree wouldn't work.

One Wednesday evening while Dad drove us home from the mid-week prayer service, I asked him if he would drop me off at our youth pastor's house.

"I need a place where I can pray and have some privacy," I told him. "I hope you understand."

He nodded and drove me to their home. I hadn't called ahead with my request, but I knew they had a room in the lower level basement away from the rest of the family. Before I knocked on the door, I hesitated. I was afraid to make my request yet not enough to walk away. Desperation and determination were my new driving force. I had to spend time in prayer that night somewhere private to hear from God. I mustered up the courage to knock.

When the pastor and his wife answered the door, I put my request before them, and they graciously welcomed me into their home. After everyone else had gone to bed and the house was quiet, I took a song book and my Bible and walked downstairs to a comfortable chair in a warm corner. Although I could no longer read, it comforted me to hold the books in my hands and turn the pages while crying out to God in prayer. From the time I was young, I memorized a Scripture verse every week of my life, and from that reserve I quoted Scriptures all night. Once again, I reminded God how he took care of the birds and clothed the lilies of the field and then told us we are more important to him than the birds and lilies—a thought so awesome, I couldn't fully comprehend it.

The hours passed as I continued to recount his promises. "And without faith it is impossible to please *Him*, for he who comes to God must believe that He is and *that* He is a rewarder of those who seek Him" (Hebrews 11:6).

"And Jesus said to him … 'All things are possible to him who believes'" (Mark 9:23). I quoted many verses that night, speaking them from my heart to God as I agonized in prayer and my tears flowed.

"I choose to believe, Lord," I cried. "I choose to trust you, though I can't see."

Night gradually gave way to the early morning hours, but the diagnosis and my future still weighed heavily on my heart. Turning the pages, I pretended to read the Bible and song book, which gave me a needed sense of comfort and normalcy. By early morning, I pretended to be in 1 Peter when, in reality, my Bible may have been in Revelation.

"Lord," I cried, "You said in First Peter 5:7 for me cast to all my cares and anxiety upon you—that you care for me. That's why I'm here, Lord. I don't know how to go on in this blindness. I don't know how to pick up the broken pieces or how to rehabilitate myself. Lord, tonight I'm laying my burden down."

I took my Bible and placed it on the floor in front of me. It represented my burden, which I laid down at the feet of Jesus. With that, the heavy weight lifted off me. Gone. I suddenly found rest for my soul, will, emotions, anxieties, and fears. Although my cheeks were wet with tears, my heart was filled with joy, and music poured out of me. "I sing because I'm happy, I sing because I'm free, for his eye is on the sparrow and I know he watches me.

I could pick up the broken pieces and go on living. Something changed within me. For I knew my God—the God who created the universe—was watching over me. As his joy overflowed within my soul, I continued my praise to him. God's peace washed over me like warm oil. His presence was there. No mistaking it. This was not an emotional experience but was supernatural. My eyes were still blind, but this was no less a miracle. His peace invaded my mind and replaced my fears.

I couldn't adequately explain it with words, but in that moment, I was set free with tangible peace. I could sing with joy and it was wonderful! The words took root in my spirit. Just as singing had worked for Paul and Silas to open the prison doors when they were imprisoned (see Acts 16:16-40), it worked for me.

I stayed in prayer until I won the victory in my soul. I could sing and let God's joy become my strength. After all, Scripture says, "Bless the LORD, O my soul, And forget none of His benefits; Who pardons all your iniquities, Who heals all your diseases; Who redeems your life from the pit, Who crowns you with lovingkindness and compassion; Who satisfies your years with good things, So *that* your youth is renewed like the eagle" (Psalm 103:2-5).

I could pray differently now. A major victory had been won, and I sensed the closeness of his presence. God instilled the courage in me to live. In order to move forward, I only needed to know how to proceed.

Before leaving my prayer room that morning, I had one final petition for the Lord.

"God," I said, "the Apostle Paul prayed that we would "be filled with the knowledge of [your] will in all spiritual wisdom and understanding" (Colossians 1:9, pronoun change by author). That means you want to reveal your will to me. Father, I don't know how to pick up the broken pieces. I don't know how to rehabilitate and pull my life back together. Lord, show me what to do."

As I waited quietly, God spoke to me. Gently but surely, he slipped something in my heart that showed me what to do next.

4

Choosing To Trust

Upon returning home, I typed a letter to the president of Tennessee Temple University, Dr. Lee Roberson, asking permission to enroll. I explained to him that though I couldn't see to read textbooks or write exams, I would be able to do my work by recording class lectures on tapes and listening to them. With fresh hope and purpose, I dropped the letter in the mail and prayed the response from Dr. Roberson would be positive.

But inside I knew. If God put it in my heart, then he would come through, and I would join my twin sister, Carolyn, in school. Oh, how I missed her.

Two weeks after mailing the letter, I received a response from Dr. Roberson. "We've never had a blind student," he wrote. "This is a new adventure for us as well. We'll take you on probation for the first semester on one condition." He went on to write that before enrolling, I'd have to ask each professor if they'd be willing to administer oral tests for me. Of course, this would mean an added responsibility for them. Further, they would have to cover all the material in the classroom discussions since I couldn't read the books, and Braille wasn't an option for me at this point.

As it turned out, the professors were more than willing to assist me, and I was cleared to start classes in January, less than three months away.

Because I was now positive that going to college was the Lord's will, I believed everything would work out. While a bit scared in moving forward with my future, I was more scared to remain where I was. Like any young person, I wanted to fulfill my dreams and goals. In many ways, I could've taken the easy road and cancel my plan to attend college, especially one six hundred fifty miles away from home. Yet, I knew this was a school where the Word of God was taught with every class lecture, and I needed that. I couldn't sit back and wait on God to deliver me from my blindness. Life had to go on in spite of it.

People often asked me, "Weren't you angry at God for making you blind? Didn't you hate him?"

No, I wasn't angry with God. He'd walked and talked with me since childhood. God didn't make me blind. This was merely a result of living in this fallen, broken world. I needed him at this time of my life more desperately than I'd needed him before. He was there for me, loving and protecting me. Like a hen gathers her chicks under her wings, God gathered me under his wings. I learned to trust him now more than ever.

I read once where Helen Keller was asked, "Is there anything worse than being blind?"

"The most pathetic person in the world," she replied, "is someone with sight and no vision."

Her response gave me comfort. I might not have sight, but God gave me a vision for my life. All I had to do was trust him one day at a time, one small step at a time.

5

Sometimes You Need A Little Help

I wasn't completely blind, but I was far more than just legally blind, I was caught between a sighted world and a completely dark world. First, I didn't look blind to the average person. Because my eyes didn't show the blindness, people didn't often recognize it. On top of that, I tried my best to hide the fact, which didn't always work—like times when I bumped into things or when walking up and down stairs and griping the railing to make my way for fear of falling forward.

I quickly discovered I was missing about half of every conversation with the loss of my sight. So much of our conversations include facial expressions and physical gestures. Other areas I'd often taken for granted concerned normal changes in society such as new construction signs that gave critical information and television advertisements. Hair, clothing, and makeup, was something I could never be sure of.

Even the slightest daily changes created problems. People would inadvertently move chairs, for example, and I'd bump into them. Or they'd leave shoes and other things laying around, and I'd trip over them. Something as seemingly insignificant as salt and pepper shakers that didn't get put back where they usually were kept became lost to me.

I slowly began to understand why the doctor, when he first explained to me that my condition was permanent, chose words that seemed so harsh. *Go home and learn to live with it.*

Yes, it was hard to hear, but he was right. I had to tackle my life-altering challenge. Blindness was a greater adversity than I'd ever faced, but I had to accept the truth and rebuild my life anew. Sugar coating the reality would have done nothing. Being a determined person didn't excuse me from needing a lot of help.

During times of crisis, everyone needs friends around. I was blessed with great friends in my hometown and church who stood beside me with their prayers. I was so thankful for that. While I knew they were talking with Mom and Dad about our visit to Mayo Clinic and the doctor's diagnosis, no one approached me personally about it, much like on my car ride home with my mother after the doctor gave us no hope. No one seemed willing to discuss it with me.

How I longed for the opportunity to open up and share my deepest fears and feelings with someone about what happened to me. I needed to know someone cared enough to come to me and ask. I now realize that most people probably didn't know what to say, and that's why they remained distant. My blurry bubble isolated me from them.

Then one day, God answered my prayer and cry of desperation when Ruth Bos, a godly mother of four high school and college age children, approached me at church. She had gone out of her way on two occasions prior to this to ask me how I was handling the challenges and gave me a listening ear.

"Marolyn, would you like to attend a women's conference at Moody Bible Institute next month?" she asked.

Her compassion touched me deeply, and I was thrilled she invited me to attend the conference with her. This would give me the opportunity to restore some activity and fellowship in my life—exactly what I needed. I'll never forget the impact she made in my life during that time. When others avoided me, Ruth went the second mile to show me she cared. I'm sure others cared too and were praying for me, but I greatly appreciated Ruth's willingness to cross over into my unseeing world.

I was also grateful for the men from the Holland Lions Club who told me about Braille watches and white canes I could purchase from the State Rehabilitation Center for the blind. How I looked forward to getting a watch. I'd be able to tell time once again.

But the cane was another issue. The Lion's Club members had purchased one for me and gave up their time to drive out into the country to bring it to me. I deeply appreciated their desire to want to do this, but carrying the cane repeatedly announced my blindness, setting me apart as handicapped. I wasn't ready for that. This way of life was new to me. I suppose in some way I was still trying to hide the fact I couldn't see—as if I could hide it. Immediately after their visit, I contacted the State Rehabilitation Center to order one of the watches.

Around that same time, I met Mr. Oliver White.

Mr. Oliver, as I referred to him, had been assigned by the State Rehabilitation for the Blind to evaluate and help the blind living in Allegan County. After the initial consultation, he visited once a month to assist me with adapting emotionally to life without sight in a seeing world. I looked forward to his visits.

He provided me with a much-needed outlet to talk about my frustrations, challenges, and fears and to work through the emotional trauma of blindness. Mr. Oliver offered to open the door for me to learn Braille and become a Dictaphone typist in a government office.

Knowing I could learn a trade to support myself encouraged me, but I was also still trying to deal with the reality that I would be blind for the rest of my life. In my state of mind, I wasn't yet able to consider the opportunity that was offered me. I needed some time for psychological adjustment and to try to pursue an academic education. I knew I'd eventually have to receive training at the Training Center for Adult Blind, but I wasn't ready yet. For now, my heart was set on attending Tennessee Temple University.

6

FREEDOM

The weeks before I left for college were consumed in a blur of preparation. Being blind, I had so many things to consider as I geared up to move out on my own. Often, I needed an escape to get away from it all, but because of my limited mobility, sometimes even the farm felt like a prison. I missed the simple freedom that came from things like riding a bike through the countryside, driving, and going roller skating on Friday nights.

Shopping now became impossible. Whomever I went shopping with needed to tell me what was available on the racks and the colors of each item or piece of clothing. I never trusted others' taste in clothing to be the same as mine. Even then I couldn't know for certain if a garment was right for me. Just because it felt good didn't mean it looked good on me.

Feeling fabric to know the style of clothing left me frustrated, so I quickly put an end to that. I was comfortable with the clothing I had. Something new might be a disaster. I'd leave for school with the clothes I had.

Blindness affected more than my sight. My life was shattered, my dreams crushed, and no words could describe my fear of the unknown. Though I now knew God was with me, I would often become overwhelmed with despair. How would I ever make it through life alone? The future could only be hopeless.

Inactivity—both physically and mentally—concerned me, and at times, I could feel myself wasting away. Of course, I played the piano, and that helped tremendously. When I was young, I'd taken piano lessons. Thank God for that. Now I was thankful for the investment of that time and for the ability to play the songs I had committed to memory. How comforting to sit and play the songs of faith and meditate on the words which had become a balm of healing for me. But I needed more. I had to do something other than sit around.

This meant becoming intentional about adding physical activity back into my life, which wasn't an easy task for me as a blind person. Fortunately, a recreational area close to my mother's work had trampolines with the mat at ground level. During that time, trampoline jump centers were all the rage. And it was perfect for me. Mom could drop me off, and though I needed to be careful, exact sight wasn't required to participate. The trampolines were ringed by safety pads, and I simply needed to be aware of border areas, which I could vaguely make out.

I was grateful for the opportunity and went there frequently. Jumping in the open air gave me a sense of freedom lost in almost every other area of my life. With each bounce, my mind opened up and allowed me to ponder my future in Bible College.

The months of adjustment to life as a blind person passed quickly before I left for Chattanooga and Tennessee Temple. Even though I had high expectations as I left, I was extremely apprehensive about this huge step forward into the unknown. I questioned myself as to whether I could handle new surroundings, but I wouldn't know unless I tried. I'd rather fail trying than not to try at all. I believed the promises of God for my future, and with his help, I expected to see them fulfilled. I believed God would help me adjust to campus life and obtain my education.

But I had a lot of big adjustments to make in life. I didn't really know if I would be strong enough to undertake such odds.

7

Never Quit

Unlike friends who knew me in Holland, the students and faculty at Tennessee Temple University didn't know I had recently lost my eyesight; and therefore, they treated me as if I'd been blind for years. I think if I'd made it known my blindness was so new to me, their sympathy would've become an even greater obstacle in my adjustment. So, initially, I didn't mention it to anyone.

At that point in my life, I was still sensitive and self-conscious about it and didn't want to talk about it or let people see the overwhelming emotional struggle weighing heavily upon me. Most of the students and faculty were strangers to me, so I figured if I didn't say anything to anyone about my blindness being recent, I might get through each day without emotionally cracking up in front of someone. Later, I would often go to my dorm room and bawl my eyes out to release all my pent-up emotions.

Each morning when I awoke, I had to make a conscious decision how I'd move forward as a blind person. Would I be a victim or a victor? Would I live in faith or in fear? I'd heard a saying, "The achievement of our goal is assured the moment we commit ourselves to it." I had to adjust my thinking regarding the obstacles I'd face that day and determine to trust God. The choices were mine.

"Lord," I often prayed, "if I must be blind, please let it be for a purpose." I'd been taught about the miracles Jesus did when he walked on earth but not about faith healing in the way that I understand it today, yet I knew God didn't make me blind. Jesus never went around making people sick. He came to give us an abundant life. The Bible declares God will make all things work together for the good for those who love him. (See Romans 8:28). As far as I was concerned, "all things" included my blindness.

Now, it's important to recognize that we do have a real enemy, a thief that comes 'to steal and kill and destroy.'

Jesus countered that fact with, "I came that they may have life, and have *it* abundantly" (John 10:10). He also said, "In the world you have *tribulation*" (John 16:33, emphasis by author).

Webster defines tribulation as misfortune, trials, suffering, pain, distress, trouble, and problems. Jesus wasn't being a pessimist. He was being a realist. In that same verse, he said, "but take courage; I have overcome the world" or our tribulation— whatever form it takes. Could I believe Jesus for abundant life? Was it possible to be of good cheer when life was upside down and nothing made sense? Of course. Otherwise, Jesus wouldn't have said it. Again, the choices were mine. I chose to trust him one day at a time as I prayed and believed him for my healing.

But adjusting to my disability, as well as taking on new surroundings like learning the campus, sidewalks, doorways, stairs, water fountains, and which were the front and back ends of the classrooms, was much harder than I thought it would be. Yet, I also recognized these challenges would be opportunities to build my faith. I was pursuing God's leading and was excited about being on campus, and in just a couple days classes would begin.

Fear of the unknown rose quickly, and I questioned my decision to leave the familiar surroundings of the house I grew up in to peruse my future. Fear of being blind in surroundings that I had never seen with my eyes. While at home, I could visualize my settings—the furniture and room layout. This was all new. I lived in a room I had never seen. What had I gotten myself into? How did I ever think I could handle this? The task before me was great—far greater than I had imagined it would be.

Like my mom always said, "When there is a will, there is a way. Figure it out." I had to take control of my thoughts and move forward with my life. My future was at stake. It wasn't easy. Satan tried to defeat me. Determined I pressed into the situation telling myself "with God all things are possible" (Mathew 19:26), and "I can do all things through Him who strengthens me" (Philippians 4:13). Sometimes when I would go down in despair, these verses became my daily meditations.

I would survive as long as I didn't quit. The school president, Dr. Roberson, often encouraged us with the words, "Young people, don't be quitters." I took his words personally. Sitting in those chapel services, I couldn't see his face, but in my mind, he was looking directly at me, speaking directly to my heart. He drilled that message into us, and it resonated in my spirit as I embarked on my uphill journey. I made the decision early on that no matter how steep my climb, I wouldn't quit. If the enemy could get me to quit, he'd win.

I buried myself in my studies—a good and healthy escape from focusing on my circumstances. The campus had a prayer tower, and I often went there so I could be alone with the Lord to pray and draw strength from God. Frequently, when other students occupied the prayer room, I went into another building on campus where not a soul was around—only Jesus and me. I relied on the peace I drew from these times alone with him in the midst of my storm as I adjusted to my new life.

My learning curve was steep as I reviewed each day's lectures through the tape-recorded sessions. For that too, I went off to a vacant room on the second floor in one of the buildings where I could be alone. Listening to and studying from the taped lectures consumed a lot of my time. To learn the material simply from hearing it spoken was difficult. I never realized until then how much we learn and take in through the gift of sight and being able to write things down for later study.

The professors gave all my exams to me orally—both an intimidating and frustrating experience. I wasn't off to the side with the teacher. Instead, as they administered the verbal test to me, other students constantly came and went or stood around waiting to speak with the professors. All that interference and those side-conversations distracted me and interrupted my thought processes. Yet, even in that I found God could use it for my good as it caused me to focus more and study harder, resulting in a 3.8 grade point average.

8

A Supernatural Vision

At the age of nine, I read the verse that says, "*You must be born again*" (John 3:7) through which God spoke to me regarding my need for the forgiveness of my sin. From the time I was young, I heard him speaking to me and calling me to himself time and time again.

I had such a longing in my heart. I desperately wanted to be "born again" into the family of God, but I didn't dare walk the aisle in church and tell the preacher about it. What would I say to the preacher? This actually went on for months. Finally, I gathered up the courage to tell my mom about my desire to accept Jesus Christ as my Lord and Savior.

She led me to a Scripture we read together. "For God so loved the world, that He gave His only begotten Son, that whoever believes in Him shall not perish, but have eternal life" (John 3:16). She asked me to place my name in the "whoever" part of the verse.

So, I prayed, "If I, Marolyn, would believe in him (Jesus Christ), I, Marolyn, would not perish but have eternal life."

As my mother knelt with me in front of the sofa in prayer that day, she joined with me as I prayed in faith, believing. I repented of my sin and asked Jesus to come into my life. In that moment, he forgave me and made me his child. I knew I was different. The Spirit of God came alive in me. I was born into the family of God in that instant.

I discovered that eternal life was God's free grace gift of his unmerited favor. All I had to do was receive it by faith. Then I took another step. Out of gratitude for what Christ has done for me, I devoted myself fully to him.

"He who has My commandments and keeps them is the one who loves Me; and he who loves Me will be loved by My Father, and I will love him and will disclose Myself to him" (John 14:21). But now that he had my heart, this was not a sacrifice but a longing. I wanted wholeheartedly to obey my Lord and walk in ways that pleased him. I've never regretted my decision.

That evening, after I accepted Jesus as my Lord and Savior, I rode my bike around the barnyard to work up the courage to tell my four older brothers what I'd done. Some may find that funny. But because I was shy, I had reservations about approaching them regarding this. It took courage. Yet, I wanted to celebrate by sharing with them the joy that now filled my heart.

God continued speaking to me after that night. I became tuned in to hear his voice because I was listening for it.

From an early age while attending elementary school, I had a close relationship with God. Once the little two-room, red-brick Sunny Side School dismissed, we walked the mile and a half back home. My brothers and sisters would head straight to the kitchen to get a snack.

Instead, I would climb the stairs, rush up to my room, drop to my knees, and talk with God. I could hardly wait to meet with him. "God, I'm home. I'm here, Lord," I'd call out, still breathless from the walk.

I'd stay there until I felt his presence, and he wrapped his arms around me. If I heard someone coming up the stairs, I immediately stopped what I was doing. I would've been embarrassed for someone to find me kneeling in prayer. I don't know why I felt that way, but I did. This was a necessary time for me ... for my heart. I needed to tell God I was home, and I wasn't satisfied to walk downstairs to join my siblings in a snack before starting our chores until I'd been wrapped in God's love.

As I've grown older, I recognize that when I sense the Lord's presence, as I did when I was a child coming home from school, instead of leaving my prayer spot, I should stay and wait quietly for him to speak to me. These times are precious and need to be treasured. I was in the presence of the most Holy God. At that time, I was young and didn't fully understand God's ways, but I longed for his presence. I fell back on the strength of this relationship when tragedy struck.

Like I mentioned earlier, there were several special places around the farm where I'd go and linger in a spirit of prayer. His presence always seemed so near. One day when I was twelve years old, I sat in my favorite prayer spot on the lawn under the clotheslines at our home. The sun was setting, the sky awash with golden color as I gazed across our acreage. The crops were ripe for harvest, and the green trees waved in the breeze.

Peace enveloped me as I took in the beauty. My heart swelled in adoration and praise to my Lord and Savior. I always marveled at God's handiwork in nature.

All of a sudden, God gave me a vision of my future. Everything around me disappeared as a movie rolled in my head. In the vision, I clearly saw that I would become a minister's wife and would speak before great audiences around the world. I was startled and shook up over what I'd seen.

"No. No, it can't be!" I balked as I thought on how my pastor's wife taught the adult ladies' Sunday school class and spoke at banquets. I could never do that. Yet, God was showing me I would speak around the world to huge audiences?

"Lord, there's no way," I cried.

I never went back to pray under the clothes lines again. What I saw in the vision frightened me. I told no one. From then on, I prayed under the one-hundred-year-old maple on the other side of the house. I hoped the Lord wouldn't bring up the vision again. In my youthful understanding, I didn't grasp that when the Lord calls his children to do something special, he also gives them the ability to do it. There's nothing to fear.

Much to my dismay, God didn't leave it alone. Again, during my prayer time alone with him under the tree one day, the vision returned. "All right Lord," I said. "I'll be a preacher's wife, and I'll be the best pastor's wife I can be, but you just leave that public speaking to somebody else!"

In my naïveté, I thought God was pleased with this agreement. I was at least willing to do one of the things he requested. So, from then on, I prayed differently as I submitted to the plan he placed before me—to be a minister's wife.

During that same year, I heard Dr. Billy Graham preaching on the radio. One of his comments resonated in my heart.

"Young people, you may only be thirteen years of age, but now is the time to begin praying for your life partner." I was twelve years old.

When I heard that statement, I was convinced God was speaking directly to me through Dr. Graham.

As I sat under the old maple tree later that day, I began praying for my husband-to-be. I figured the guy I would marry might be thirteen at that time. I prayed he would be a man of God; that he would love God with all his heart, soul and mind; and that he would be a man of prayer. I also prayed God would protect him from the evil is in this world and keep him pure and holy throughout his teenage life. I prayed for practical things as well, that he would love me dearly; that he would be kind, compassionate, tender, and understanding; and that our lives would be interwoven so we would have a joint ministry for the Lord.

I never gave any more thought about speaking around the world. God and I had an agreement regarding that.

Some people say, "I don't believe one can actually hear God speaking."

I don't agree with that statement. God tells us, "Your ears will hear a word behind you, 'This is the way, walk in it'" (Isaiah 30:21). For me, the word *it* refers to the Scriptures I read in which God speaks to my heart and gives instruction. It also refers to those impressions God lays on my spirit.

9

GOD SPEAKS AGAIN

At Tennessee Temple, I was grateful for the new relationships and friendships being built. The first semester in which my sister Carolyn attended classes before I arrived, she met a freshmen student named Hersholt Ford. He had a brother, Acie, and sister, Hazel, who also attended Temple.

Prior to my starting in January, I had the opportunity to visit the campus and my sister in November over Thanksgiving week. That was the first time I had the opportunity to meet Hersholt, Acie, and their sister, Hazel. They were very friendly and immediately welcomed me.

Hersholt turned to his brother and said, "Hey, Acie. Would you mind showing Marolyn around the campus?"

"Sure," Acie said, sounding happy to help.

Like a gentleman, Acie gave me a tour around the campus. Afterward, I learned he hadn't wanted to, but because I was blind, he agreed to it. Later that evening, we all met together in the "dating parlor," the one place on campus reserved for male and female interactions. I enjoyed the evening and cherished the new friendships. I especially liked Acie.

He must have felt the same way because the next morning, he sat with me at breakfast.

"You make this place cheerier," he said.

"I do?" I said, smiling.

"Yeah." He cleared his throat. "So … what are you doing Friday night?"

"Ah … I don't know."

"Would you like to go to the basketball game on Friday?"

Shocked at his question, I paused a moment. I'm not sure what went faster, my mind or my heart. He wanted to ask *me*, a blind girl, on a date?

"I'd love to," I finally answered.

At the game that night, my heart fluttered the whole time. I hadn't dated anybody since I'd gone blind. Acie took me to the game because none of us had any money, and students got in free. But I didn't care where it was. A guy asked me for a date! Neither of us cared about the game. We were together. I felt a chemistry between us … that special spark. I could still see people's fuzzy outlines and could walk around them. Acie took my hand and gently guided me up the bleachers to our seats.

The next morning, he sat with me again for breakfast and lunch, and then at every meal for the rest of the week. The more we learned about each other, the more I sensed something extra special about him. Acie had every characteristic I'd asked God to place in the man I would marry—tender, loving, kind, compassionate, and understanding. His love for God was deep and real. And he had depth of character. Could he possibly be *the one*? The future husband I'd been praying for since I was twelve? I chuckled to myself. As the week progressed, though, I clearly sensed the Lord speaking to my heart.

Marolyn, this is the man you have been praying for all these years.

It came from the Lord. After years together, I knew God's voice. Joy burst inside me, but I knew enough to keep quiet. God alone would have to confirm this possibility to Acie.

GOD SAID YES!

I returned home during the month of December. Acie and I exchanged letters. Through our correspondence, I got to know more about him—his likes and dislikes, his hobbies. What's funny is I could write letters because I was an accomplished typist, but I couldn't read his letters. I had to find someone to read them to me. No way was I going to let my Mom read my love letters, so I had to find a friend I could trust.

Although I would have loved to have had long phone conversations with Acie and Carolyn—oh, how I missed her—we didn't have cell phones with perks like unlimited minutes back then. Long distance calls were expensive, and we shared a party line with seven other neighbors. Yes, they listened in on everybody's calls. Long distance calls were only for critical things, short and to the point conversations. Letter writing was our main mode of long-distance communication, and we did it weekly. "Stamps have gone up to five cents," Mom said, so we couldn't write daily.

The month passed quickly, and soon the time came for me to start college and venture out on my own. The second semester was scheduled to begin in a few days, so with great anticipation and a dusting of hesitation, I returned to the campus. I was looking forward to once again being with my twin, but I have to admit, I was also looking forward to seeing someone special.

Acie and I picked up right where we left off ... sort of. Imagine dating someone you couldn't see. Of course, Carolyn filled me in on those details. She assured me that Acie was a good-looking guy.

"He's perfect for you," she told me. "He's handsome, walks straight, and holds his head up—very successful looking."

I also heard other girls talking about how handsome he was and that he had rosy cheeks, dark hair, and beautiful green eyes. I couldn't see any of that, but that's not what drew me to him. I fell in love with his spirit. He had all the qualities I asked God to put in the man I would marry—a tender spirit and a deep love for people. He was kind, loyal, and faithful to his work and had the ability to analyze problems and develop solutions. He operated in the *gift of mercy* which was evidenced in the way he treated those around him. This endeared him to me.

The first night on campus in January, Acie and I sat in the dating parlor. I'd purchased a small gift for him before leaving home—a tie clasp, which I planned on giving him when I arrived. We sat and talked that night, and as I was about to give him the gift, he told me he had his eye on a girl he wanted to ask out. The moment he spoke her name, she walked into the parlor.

"There she is now," he said.

My heart was crushed. And yet, to my dismay, I encouraged him to date her. If and when we ever started dating more seriously, I didn't want him to have any reservations in his mind regarding girls he hadn't dated.

"If you have a desire to date her," I replied, "then that's what you need to do." I'd learned over the years that it's necessary to wait on God's timing.

The Scripture that strengthened me during that time was, "Delight yourself in the Lord; and He will give you the desires of your heart" (Psalm 37:4). I went ahead and gave him the gift, and he was grateful. But I was bummed. I'd been certain Acie was the man who God said was to be my husband, and while difficult to watch him date someone else, I chose to trust God.

Fortunately, I didn't have to wait long. After only one date with that other girl, Acie and I were back together again.

Acie

GOD SAID YES!

Acie's life continually inspired me. He'd dedicated his life to Jesus when he was ten years old, and from that time on he had a burning passion for prayer and intimate fellowship with his Lord. Even at that young age, he recognized God was calling him for a purpose, although at the time, he didn't completely understand the specifics.

One day during the summer following his high school graduation, he was driving around with his friend, Phil Rogers. Acie had already preregistered at Louisiana State University where Phil had attended the previous year. But instead of experiencing the typical feelings of anticipation, Acie was troubled in his spirit. The more he tried to shake the feeling, the more concerned he became. During this time of searching, Acie had carefully chosen friends who helped build his faith and challenged his spiritual walk.

As they were out driving together that day, Acie turned to Phil and said, "I'm enrolled at LSU, but I believe God wants something different for me. I have this uneasiness in my spirit."

"You need to obey God, Acie," Phil replied.

Acie believed he must allow the Holy Spirit to lead him in life and not be led by his flesh. He could have ignored the feeling of uneasiness that now pricked his heart, but he chose instead to listen to the inner prompting of the Holy Spirit, to seek guidance. So, he shared what he was feeling with Phil. Years before, he'd chosen Proverbs 3:5-6 as his life verse. "Trust in the Lord with all your heart, and do not lean on your own understanding. In all your ways acknowledge Him, and he will make your paths straight."

Once Acie realized the Holy Spirit was prompting him, a dam broke, and he knew in his heart God had something else in store. He trusted the Holy Spirit to guide him for this next step in his future. But to where? Certainly not LSU.

That night Phil and Acie approached Phil's father, Rev. W. R. Rogers, with the situation.

Rev. Rogers wasn't only Phil's father, but he was also Acie's pastor and someone he respected immensely. Under his ministry, Acie had been mentored and now, felt a call to preach. As Acie shared with him his hesitation in continuing to pursue his present course, Rev. Rogers shared with him about Tennessee Temple College in Chattanooga, Tennessee.

Not long after this talk, a supernatural peace and a strong desire to attend college at Tennessee Temple soon replaced the feeling of discontent that had plagued his previous decision to attend LSU. He sensed that by attending Tennessee Temple he could prepare himself for the call the Lord placed on his heart to be a minister of the gospel. Immediately, he applied to Tennessee Temple, was accepted, and subsequently enrolled in September.

He didn't have a dime to his name, didn't have a job, and had no way of paying the tuition and other necessary expenses. But he had an unshakable faith. Acie believed that where God guides, he provides. He returned to the strength of his life verse to trust in the Lord.

His persistence and work ethics paid off, and the week after classes began, he landed a job working as a clothing salesman the week after classes began.

Thomas Edison once quipped, "Opportunity is missed by most people because it is dressed in overalls and looks like work."

Acie didn't have that problem. He took this job opportunity as another confirmation that he was exactly where God wanted him.

10

Things Get Real

My first semester exams were facing me, and I felt the pressure to go into hyper-study mode and start an early review of my lecture recordings. Studying from the recordings took longer because of all the stopping and rewinding.

"My parents are coming to visit," Acie informed me.

Not the best timing, yet I was flattered he asked me to meet them.

Though we'd grown close, we hadn't made a commitment and were still dating others ... sort-of. In our spirits, we pretty much knew we'd end up together, but we weren't ready to formally commit. Both of us wanted to make absolutely sure. His asking me to meet his parents was a big sign to me.

While I'd been praying for my life partner since the age of twelve, I also had been praying for my in-laws. I wanted them to love and accept me and for us to have a sweet relationship. With what I felt in my heart for Acie, I greatly anticipated and welcomed the opportunity to get to meet his parents.

It didn't surprise me, but I fell in love with Willard and Virginia Ford. Like Acie, they were humble and had a deep love for people and for God. Even though they were visiting Acie, Hersholt, and Hazel, they wanted to visit with me as well.

Apparently, Acie had told them about me. They invited me to dinner with them and readily drew me into conversation like

DR. MAROLYN FORD

I was already part of the family. My blindness didn't seem to be an issue for them. In fact, they never mentioned it.

Before they left, I had no doubt they completely accepted me and loved me, blindness and all. What parent would want their son to marry a blind girl? But it didn't bother them. To me, that was further proof God had control of the situation. How could it be mere coincidence? I had no doubt in my mind that God orchestrated the entirety of my meeting Acie and his family.

After Acie saw his parents' acceptance of me, we began to get more serious. Still, both of us occasionally dated others, but we were mostly going through the motions. He had a hard time formally committing, but then something happened that jolted him to reality.

Someone else asked me to marry him.

I couldn't believe it. I'd casually gone out with this guy a couple times. The whole time we were on our dates, I thought about Acie. I simply saw this other guy as a friend, but it made me question all over again why anyone would want to marry me, a blind girl. What was it about me that would make someone love me so much that my blindness didn't matter?

Of course, I never considered marrying this other guy, but the proposal did turn out to be from God. When Acie learned of the proposal, he came running and poured out his true feelings to me. He'd dragged his feet toward commitment and dated other girls because he'd been concerned and wanted to be sure that what he felt for me was truly love and not pity. Although difficult, I needed to hear it.

From then on, our relationship became serious. We opened up and discussed in depth how my blindness would impact our marriage.

Even with glasses, the best correctable visual acuity the doctor was able to attain for me was 7/200, and 14/224 vision.

GOD SAID YES!

According to the Snellen Visual Acuity chart, my worst eye had a 92.8% loss of eyesight. The doctor then explained that my best eye meant that a word that most people could read at two hundred hundred feet away was visible to me at seven feet away. With what little sight I had, I could only make out vague outlines of objects. Details were a thing of the past. Add to that the prognosis that I would eventually lose what tiny bit of sight I did have. If we married, ours wouldn't be a typical marriage, and we needed to face those challenges head on.

Could I be an adequate wife and mother? I'd already learned to navigate a college campus and was pursuing my degree. My grades were good, and I was adjusting to the fact that I was blind. I'm a type-A personality—the kind of person who believes I can do anything if I try.

The more Acie and I talked, the more I became convinced I could do anything I set my mind to do. Being a wife and mother was one more challenge I knew I could conquer, especially with God's power residing inside me. I was learning to lean on his strength for each step—day by day.

But did Acie really believe that? Could I be a helpmate to him and not a burden? As he grasped the full weightiness of my long-term situation, would he back out? If he did, I'd be hurt but wouldn't blame him. Really, who wants to marry a blind girl? I still hadn't fully accepted it.

11

Eight months had passed since I received the marriage proposal from the other young man on campus, and Acie and I grew more serious in our commitment and discussions with each other. We talked through every possible scenario facing us, and Acie was all in. We dated for another year. He now knew his heart, and we were both assured marriage was God's plan for us.

One night, we were sitting on the brick wall at the front entrance to the Highland Park Campus church. "I think we're supposed to get married," he said. His proposal was more of an ongoing conversation.

It came as no surprise because we'd been talking about marriage for some time, but this proposal came unexpectedly for me. Wow! I loved him so much, my heart leapt within me. He was asking me to marry him.

"I know we are." I replied excitedly. I was thrilled God actually had a man who would marry me. My heart bubbled over with joy. This wasn't just anybody; he was someone I could be proud to introduce as my husband. Other girls were after this good-looking guy on campus. Now he would be all mine. Words could never express my joy and happiness.

Realizing rings were too expensive for our tiny budget, we turned to the Service Merchandise catalog that was laying around in the campus dating parlor. We weren't the only ones on campus thinking about wedding rings. Most of the students were hard up for money and weren't able to purchase a Coke at the campus store, so buying rings out of the catalog was a common occurrence.

He flipped through the pages. "Here's one we can afford," he said. "Both rings are beautiful and cost $40 together." They were 14-carat gold, and the price was perfect for us.

We ordered them immediately and waited for them to arrive in the mail. Later in our marriage, Acie wanted to buy me a nicer ring, but I said, "No, this is the one I love. It's beautiful, and it's all I want."

After our engagement, I finally told Acie how the Lord spoke to me the day we first met, saying, *this is the young man you have been praying for all these years.*

"I've known it too" he replied. "But I had to confirm it."

With both our parents' blessings, we settled on an August wedding, only four months away during semester break. Because of our school schedules and the six hundred thirty miles between Tennessee and Michigan, Acie didn't get to meet my parents until two days before the wedding.

This put them at a place where they also had to trust God and me. To their credit, they never questioned our decision to marry, for which I was grateful. They didn't ask if I was sure he was the right life partner for me and whether he could support me.

If Acie was my choice, then that was fine with them. I'd written them each week while in college and told them all about Acie, which I think helped them feel they knew him and trusted him. They must have understood that it would take a special individual to want to marry their blind daughter and take care of her. Not just anyone would make a commitment of that magnitude. He had to be "one special guy."

GOD SAID YES!

Due to my blindness, my mother stepped in and worked out most of the details—the flowers, candle arrangements, and the bridesmaids' dresses. I chose the colors and made suggestions, but Mom had to be my eyes.

Acie's mother was a seamstress and offered to sew my wedding dress. I have to admit I was a little concerned when I sent her my measurements. Would it fit when the time came? I was in Chattanooga, and she lived in Louisiana, so there was no actual time for fittings to check her work on my frame. However, she assured me she was praying about every stitch she put into the dress and that it would fit and look beautiful.

She was correct. I ran my fingers over the material, discovering the intricate patterns she designed into the dress and the long flowing train. It was beautiful beyond my expectations, more than I could ever hope for. After a couple adjustments made by a seamstress in Holland, it fit perfectly. To add that traditional element of something old, she sewed Grandma's pearls one-by-one all over the train of the dress. She labored over that dress as her special gift to us, and although I couldn't see the intricate details, the compliments that others shared with me let me know it was indeed stunning.

Carolyn, my younger sister Virginia, and my friend Carol Ver Hey were bridesmaids. My three brothers stood with Acie. I shared with Mom what color and style of dresses I wanted the bridesmaids to wear, the tuxes for the groomsmen, and the flowers I preferred in the wedding décor.

Walking down the aisle, I couldn't see the face of the man waiting for me, and a curious blend of emotions besieged me—anxiety and the fear of stepping into a big commitment. I'd been away from home and not in the kitchen learning how to cook without sight. This was a big step of faith on my part. I didn't know how I would be able to handle all that would be required of me, but like my mom always said, "If there's a will, there's a way." The excitement and joy of knowing I was actually getting married and could live a normal life and bear children was a God-given blessing beyond words.

When the preacher told Acie, "You may kiss your bride," I aimed for where I thought his lips were and kissed the side of his face. Acie chuckled and calmly moved his lips to mine. What an incredible gift God gave me.

I expected a small reception following the wedding, but Mom and Dad had their own special contribution to our wedding. They surprised me with a full five-course reception dinner for our guests at the Warm Friend Hotel in Holland, Michigan—a formal, elegant affair. Mom filled me in on what Dad wanted for the reception. She and I together choose the decorations for the tables—white linen tablecloths and white candles lit on each table with red carnations.

Acie and I decided together that my brother Don and his wife, Clara, would be our master and mistress of ceremony. They'd play their instruments and preside over the program. The seventy-five guests all came dressed in suits and dresses, and the master and mistress of ceremony played their instruments and put on a fantastic program.

Before the three-tier cake—decorated with a bride and groom on the top, with pink flowers and green leaves—was cut, Acie and I went to the tables and greeted the guests, giving each a Hershey Almond candy bar as a thank you for coming. The dinner started with a cup of soup and salad followed by their choice of ribeye steak or chicken.

After the reception, we got into our borrowed, dark-green Buick with tin cans streaming behind and headed for Canada—a six- to eight-hour drive from Holland. We'd been driving about an hour when our car broke down at one a.m. in Grand Rapids. We walked to a nearby motel and banged on the office door to awaken the office manager, but no one answered.

A hippie fellow in one of the motel rooms heard our knocking and opened his door to see what the commotion was all about. As we shared our dilemma, he explained he was finished with his room and offered it to us if we wanted it since it was already paid for through morning. We chuckled a little inwardly and declined his offer. We asked him if he knew where we could get a tow to get our car repaired.

"I know of one that's open all night," he said, nodding. "I'll drive you there." This was back in the day when people were trustworthy and helpful. Neither Acie nor I were worried about receiving help and getting in a car with a complete stranger.

True to his word, the hippie drove us to an all-night repair shop, dropped us off, and waved good-bye. The mechanic then drove us back out to our stranded vehicle in his tow truck.

Prior to leaving the reception hall after the wedding, I'd changed into my going-away outfit—a navy and white dress with a corsage, with white hat, gloves, and shoes. Much to my dismay, the tow truck was big and dirty and so high off the ground that Acie had to pick me up and put me into the cab. Never would I have imagined our wedding night would turn out like this.

Our car was finally hoisted onto the wrecker around two a.m. The mechanic was kind enough to drive the short distance over to the motel and wait while Acie obtained a room for us. I stayed at the motel while Acie and the mechanic went to the repair shop with the car on the wrecker. Neither of us expected to spend our first night as husband and wife separated from one another.

Finally, at three o'clock in the morning, the car was repaired, Acie paid the bill, and headed to the motel. But in an unfamiliar area, not having ever driven in a big city with expressways going in all directions, he got lost.

Tired and frustrated, he stopped and asked for directions. He finally made it to the room around four o'clock. Exhausted, he reached for his pajamas and found that as a practical joke, the seamstress at the men's clothing store where he worked had sewn the sleeves and legs shut in tiny machine stitches. Being blind, I wasn't much help, and he didn't know how to find the main thread and pull out the stitches. So, we sat trying to release the thread one stitch at a time before crawling into bed. What a night!

Morning came way too soon, but although we got only a few hours of sleep, we decided to get up and proceed to Ontario, to begin our honeymoon as originally planned.

Unfortunately, once we arrived, we discovered the unexpected car repair combined with the high tourist rates for the motel, food, and gas in Canada were more than we could now afford. So, after making the journey into Canada, we had to turn right around and cross back over into the US to get a motel. As we reached the ferry that would carry us across the border into the US, we discovered cars lined up four abreast, also awaiting their turn to go across. Once our car was positioned in the lineup to board the ferry, we couldn't leave our car to go anywhere. We had to wait an additional two hours in the heavy rain before we finally boarded. Our honeymoon had certainly become an exercise in patience, but at least we were together.

Finally, we were ferried across. We were tired and immediately searched for an overdue rest stop. We drove for miles without seeing a gas station, restaurant, or motel. We were working off just a few hours of sleep and had experienced another frustrating day. All we wanted was to find a motel, get some food, and rest.

When we became dead tired and simply couldn't go any further, we saw a sign that read "twenty miles to the next motel." With expectation that our long journey was almost over for the day and the hope of a good meal, we pressed through. However, when we arrived, we discovered only a small roadside inn without a restaurant or anything nearby, not even a gas station. After a quick inquiry, we were told the nearest restaurant and gas station was another hour's drive from there.

Too tired to drive another fifty miles, we chose sleep over food, booked a room, and went to bed hungry.

The next morning, Acie summed up what we were both feeling with the comment, "Let's go back to your mama's so we can get a good night's sleep and some good food."

We chose the route that took us through Upper Michigan and were delighted to see the area had a lot to offer tourists. So, we had fun stopping and sightseeing on the route back. Being together overshadowed all the trouble we experienced on the trip. Our love, warm smiles, and stolen kisses overrode any disappointment we could have felt.

Today, we can look back at those first two days of marriage and laugh at the numerous challenges we encountered when starting out on our ten-day honeymoon. But in spite of the fact we never had the "honeymoon of our dreams," we were happy to be together and remained positive.

In retrospect, our rather disappointing start to our honeymoon was a great reminder that the attitude we took toward life's circumstances was most important. Life didn't always turn out the way we expected. Our choices as to what we'd do when the unexpected circumstances occurred made all the difference in how we managed our life's journey. Attitude and joy were choices we made that weren't based on outward circumstances but on our inward relationship with God.

Our choice to not dwell on the negative in those early days only served to cement our relationship with hope for the future.

12

FAITH WITH SLEEVES ROLLED UP

After the honeymoon, we moved back to Chattanooga into a lovely second-floor apartment close enough to the campus, so we didn't need a car. In addition, the city bus stopped on the corner near our apartment and went directly to Acie's work downtown. Knowing I was blind, our landlord graciously suggested I go with her when she shopped for her weekly groceries. What a blessing!

Though money was tight, our marriage got off to a wonderful start. God had been good. We survived on Acie's salary. His parents couldn't help us financially, so he worked on his job eight hours a day and still juggled his schooling. Both of us were good at managing money and could make a dollar stretch a long way. We were as happy as two could be. Married life was a dream. Even with blind eyes, I figured out how to cook, clean, and do laundry—including ironing—and become a good partner for Acie.

A year passed, and Acie didn't have enough money to pay his school bill. He trusted God to provide for his tuition. If the money didn't come in, he wouldn't be allowed to take the final exams and would be required to retake the entire semester over. A week before the exams, he went by the financial office to see if the money had come in. It hadn't.

Each day thereafter, as exam day approached, he stopped at the financial office or at his mailbox to see if God had provided. Still nothing. He prayed fervently, standing in faith that God would bless him with a financial miracle. God answers prayers in many different ways. But more often than not, he works through other people to bring the answers.

On the morning of his first scheduled exam, he checked his mailbox one last time and found a note asking him to come by the financial office. *What could this mean? Perhaps this is my miracle?*

"Your account has been paid in full by an anonymous donor," the office assistant informed him with a smile.

Acie was able to take his exams. But more than that, the experience had built his faith that God was taking care of him and would provide for every need he had. This faith-building experience of provision for his tuition was one out of many areas in which he was learning to go deeper with God. But God was preparing him in other ways too.

One day as he was in the prayer tower on campus talking with the Lord and reading his Bible, he read, "Blessed are those who hunger and thirst for righteousness, for they shall be satisfied" (Matthew 5:6). As he read the Scripture, God filled his spirit to overflowing and confirmed again to him the call to become a minister of the gospel. Something changed in him that day that was tangible. Everyone noticed this change.

One of his professors stopped me as we passed on the sidewalk and made the comment, "Acie is a different person."

No longer timid, he spoke enthusiastically with everyone of God's greatness. An inner strength resided within him that hadn't been there before. God was preparing him for his future life as a minister of the Gospel.

And I had been called to be a minister's wife—a fulfillment of my childhood vision.

Graduation day finally came. Acie received his Bachelor of Religious Education degree from Tennessee Temple College.

Shortly after that, we drove up to Michigan to spend a few days with my family. While there, Acie heard of the Cornerstone University located in Grand Rapids, Michigan. We drove over and talked to the Dean of Students to inquire about the school. Originally, we planned to go back to Tennessee to pursue Acie's graduate studies at a university in the south, but after talking with the Dean, Acie wasn't so sure. We needed a quick answer from God for direction.

Sometimes, when we read the Bible, we didn't find a direct answer. In this case, which university to attend. Attending Cornerstone University would certainly be closer to family, but that couldn't be the basis of our decision. Yet, the more we pursued this direction of thinking for Acie's studies, the more we sensed God's peace. When we were told all his credits would transfer, that finalized our decision. Assured that this was God's plan, we moved to Grand Rapids, Michigan.

Before school started, we lived with Mom and Dad for a couple weeks until we could locate an apartment. The farm kept us busy. Acie hadn't grown up on a farm, but he rolled up his sleeves and helped as if he were one of my brothers. Mom needed to have some bushes dug up, while other bushes required a trim, and the garden needed tending to. Also, each day six- to eight-bushel baskets of eggs needed to be gathered from the chickens, washed, checked for disease, and placed in egg cartons.

With Acie's classes starting in September, we were able to locate an upstairs apartment for rent near the campus. He applied for work at several clothing stores in the area and was persistent in his follow up with these employers. We were down to the last of our money with only enough for each of us to have an ice cream cone for dinner that evening.

That day the manager of the Hausemen's Clothing Store said, "Acie, I don't need another employee, but I've never known anyone as persistent as you about finding work. You've got a job. I'll give you an advance on your first week's paycheck tomorrow morning." His employer was so thoughtful. Once again God provided for our need.

A couple months later while attending classes in Grand Rapids, Acie became the temporary interim youth pastor of the Rose Park Baptist Church in Holland, Michigan. Though a weekend position until they could get someone to work with their youth, it helped. He continued working both these jobs while working on his Bachelor of Theology degree.

During his last semester before graduation, he was advised to pastor a small church before enrolling in Seminary. So, two months after he graduated, we relocated again but this time to pastor the Bosco Baptist Church in Monroe, Louisiana. Rev. Paul Carter ordained and licensed Acie into the ministry.

13

LABOR PAINS AND BLESSINGS

We'd only been in Louisiana a short time when my Mom and Dad came down from Michigan to visit us. They'd never been to that part of the country, and even though I was having bad stomach pain when they arrived, we entertained them for a few days and did some sightseeing. Thinking it was my regular severe monthly pain, I had to grit my teeth and bear it as usual. I was determined to show them a good time and thought maybe riding in the car would help. The unbearable cramping pain began shooting down to my knees. When I couldn't handle the pain any longer, Acie cut the outing short and drove home so I could lie down.

The pain wouldn't stop. Evening came with no relief, and the night proved even worse. Concerned, Mom and Dad urged me to get to the doctor as soon as possible. I assured them I would go right away. They left early the next morning.

After we hugged and said our goodbyes, Acie rushed me to the doctor's office. Because of my distress, they kindly worked me into their schedule.

"Mrs. Ford, you're pregnant," the doctor said.

I think my jaw dropped open as a rush of joy surged through me.

"However, you are miscarrying," the doctor continued. "The cramps are actually labor pains. This is God's way of taking care of pregnancies in which there are complications."

My heart pounded heavily in my chest and tears trickled down my cheeks. *No! This can't be happening!*

"Don't worry. You're young," he encouraged. "You can try again."

Acie and I had to pick up and go on. In a way, our pain of the miscarriage, in addition to dealing with my blindness, equipped us to handle ministering to the people of our congregation who were going through deep suffering. We understood pain and loss because we'd been through so much.

One of the most difficult situations we faced as pastors in our ministry was when twin babies had been born to one of our church families. One of the twins lived, and the other died. Devastated, the family looked to us for comfort and answers. We didn't have all the answers, but we could offer comfort. Often, in times like those, words weren't much help. The most important thing we could do was stand by them and walk with them through it. And that's what we did.

Being a twin, I was deeply disturbed the one twin had died. The babies were together in the womb, and then suddenly, one was gone. As the surviving child grew, he or she would always feel that vacuum. They may not understand it, but they'd always feel something missing in their life.

Helping people through the dark days, standing by the families of the sick and dying, and preaching at funerals were the hardest tasks my husband and I ever had to do. Though challenging, God had anointed us and equipped Acie to do it well.

Acie sensed the Lord leading us back to Tennessee Temple in Chattanooga so he could attend seminary and complete his master's degree.

Once again, we stepped out in faith as we packed, not knowing where we'd live. He had no job, and we had little money. But we did have God's guidance and an overwhelming sense of peace, despite the lack of secured details. We already learned that the safest place for us—for anyone—is in obedience to God's leading. We often heard it said, "Where God guides, he provides." That didn't give us an excuse for lack of planning, but it did give us peace that while sometimes we try to get everything all planned and organized, God sometimes has another plan.

We were certain that moving back to Chattanooga for Acie to attend seminary was God's next step for us. I too was able to attend classes and pick up courses working toward my music degree.

We arrived in Chattanooga with all our possessions stuffed into an eight-foot trailer. I moved carefully, feeling my way through each day. Though my blindness made things more difficult, we did what we had to do. Struggle by struggle, we learned to adapt.

In addition, we were living on money dwindling quickly. With no idea where we'd live, we needed something inexpensive to fit our limited budget. A couple from our previous days at Temple gave us the name of a woman who rented apartments near the school. Thankfully, she had a beautiful, brand new duplex available and was willing to let us move in without a deposit or the first month's rent.

"I've learned to trust the Temple students," she informed us. "They're trustworthy and take care of my property, so I like to rent to them. Just pay me once you get your first paycheck."

Acie hadn't obtained a job yet. What a blessing from God! I couldn't see the house and wondered what it looked like in the sunlight, and then by moonlight. Each time we moved I had to reacclimate to a new home and new area. But the duplex was new and clean which made it easier for me.

With our housing taken care of, Acie again turned his sights on looking for employment. After two weeks of diligent searching, he found work as a salesman in one of the men's clothing stores in downtown Chattanooga. There he received the nickname "man of the cloth." Within two weeks after stepping out in faith to make this move, God once again provided for all our needs, reminding us of His faithfulness. We were able to pay our first month's rest on time. God was so good to us.

Time passed quickly as Acie diligently pursued his master's degree. He frequently told me, "Honey, I love the way you're always so cheerful when I come in—like you're actually glad to see me. I really like that about you."

But on one particular day when I met him, he could sense that something was up.

"Acie, I'm pregnant!" I exclaimed.

"Are you sure?" he said.

"I did a home test, and it came back positive!"

Both of us were excited, yet with cautious reservation. We had already been down this road before and never wanted to experience that sorrow again.

The doctor confirmed the test. During my pregnancy, the couple living next door were also Tennessee Temple students. She happened to be pregnant at the same time as I, only three weeks ahead of me. She was a godsend and helped me greatly. I was able to pace myself according to her experiences as we compared the progress of our pregnancies. Of course, I was anxious, not knowing how I was going to handle giving birth and being a mother.

After I married Acie, I learned how to cook without seeing the water boiling in the pan. I was apprehensive then, and I was even more apprehensive now. This was a house that could burn down if I wasn't careful, and this was where a baby would be coming into my blind world. I was so thankful for the pregnancy and praised God for it. But I thought through the process of how I would change her diapers—give her a bath, right?

I asked myself how I'd be able to find her after she began crawling. By the time she dropped out of the womb, I'd thought through every possible avenue of adventure and was anticipating her birth.

As it turned out, giving birth was the easy part. God blessed us with a healthy seven-pound, ten-ounce baby girl with no complications. Acie chose the name Sharon Marie. But after the nurse put Sharon in my arms, I sobbed. I couldn't see my baby. With tears in my eyes, I felt her little legs and arms, the shape of her body. Pulling her next to my face, I touched her tender cheek against mine and kissed her head, taking in her softness and aroma. Acie told me how beautiful she was.

"Honey, you'd love her," he said as he lovingly described her features to me—bright blue eyes and blonde hair like her mother's. I gently caressed her face and imagined in my mind how she looked from Acie's description. Oh, how I wished I could see her face for myself.

Becoming a mother was the most challenging experience I'd faced since being blind. Adding being a mother to the challenges of blindness sent me to my knees to seek the Lord for his help. Growing up in a family with several brothers and sisters, I'd always wanted a large family. I knew the benefits associated from these relationships and hoped Acie and I could have several children.

Some may find that odd. Why would I desire to have children, considering my limitations? But I recognized that children are a gift from God. I couldn't imagine how empty life would be without them. I didn't mind the extra work. The older children would teach the younger.

Acie was a huge help the first few days and weeks as we adjusted to the addition of Sharon in our lives. As she grew, I had no difficulty feeding her. All I had to do was to place my fingers around her lips, place the bottle or spoon between my fingers and pop it right into her little mouth. Babies provide a myriad of diapers that need changing, but we had plenty of water for a good bath to ensure she was always clean.

14

POTATOES!

Without a doubt, our lives were full. Acie was in his last semester in seminary, and Sharon added a richness to our lives we never imagined possible. However, that didn't mean things were always easy. As students paying tuition, rent, and providing for a baby, finances were always limited. We weren't alone as we struggled to have money left for food. Most of the Temple students were struggling financially as they worked their way toward getting their education paid for each semester.

In order to make a little more money, Acie quit his job at the clothing store and went to work at a carpet factory at night and attended classes during the day. While this job provided slightly more money, it didn't allow him to get much sleep. He maintained a back-breaking schedule, but graduation was in sight, so he worked hard to provide for us and kept up his grades.

Acie's parents decided to come from Louisiana to visit. They were scheduled to show up late the next day. Thankfully, Acie would receive his paycheck that morning so we could go out and buy groceries before they arrived. We were down to our last potato. I looked forward to seeing his parent's and was thankful the timing coordinated with payday.

The day before they were to arrive, I cleaned the house and put on a pot of water to boil the dinner of our last potato. I hummed to myself while working. That is, until I heard a car pull into our driveway.

"They're here, Acie!" I exclaimed. They'd arrived one day early. I immediately panicked. What would we do? Our cupboards were empty. I had nothing to give them.

"Acie, what are we going to do?" I asked. "We don't have any food for them tonight, and this is our last potato."

Trying to keep the alarm from my face, we greeted his parents at the door with a warm but trembling hug. I was genuinely happy they were there ... even if a day early. Mom followed me into the kitchen as I explained I was cooking. She immediately took inventory of the one potato in the pot.

I was embarrassed. "I'm so sorry, I don't have—"

"Oh, honey," she interrupted with a touch on my arm. "You wouldn't believe it. I have a bag of potatoes in the car. We had locked the house up and were out the driveway when I told Willard I needed to go back into the house to get the bag of potatoes I intended to bring. I just couldn't leave without those potatoes. I knew you'd need them. We have enough to fix some for all of us."

My heart was warmed by my mother-in-law's sensitivity to the spirit pertaining to that situation. Such love. I teared up as my heart became overwhelmed with gratitude for God's provision. I gave her a hug. She never made me feel uncomfortable. Instead, she made me feel cared for. My mother in-law was a godly and compassionate woman. She knew how to hear God's voice even in something as simple as the Holy Spirit's prompting to go back into the house for a bag of potatoes. God had once again provided for us through her simple act of obedience, which greatly impacted me.

I was reminded of a valuable lesson that day. In the practical daily aspect of our lives, we need to hear God's voice, not just in times of crisis. We hear him and know his voice from having a relationship with him. My mother-in-law spent time in God's presence so she was in tune with his voice.

God continued to show us his provision that year. We attended the Highland Park Baptist Church on campus where I was involved in a Sunday school class that planned to give a "food shower" to a needy family the day before Thanksgiving. Everyone was asked to bring canned goods to the classroom. The class planned to purchase a ham, turkey, milk, eggs, butter, potatoes and other perishable items to go with all the canned goods contributed before making the delivery. Evidently, this group reached out to the community every year.

Unfortunately, I felt uncomfortable as I came to class empty-handed each week.

Finally, with just a couple weeks left, I asked God to help me obtain something I could contribute. God answered my simple prayer. I remember thanking God for his provision as I walked into the classroom smiling and placed my donation on what felt like a mountain of canned goods. Everyone had given generously. My heart soared that we were part of something special for whatever family would receive this blessing.

Two days before Thanksgiving Day, the church volunteers set off to deliver the "shower" of food.

Imagine my surprise when they came to our door. I couldn't believe it! The Sunday school class had seen our need, and God once again provided for us through our Christian family. I was so grateful it left me speechless. With tear-filled eyes, I gave them all big hugs, repeatedly saying thank you. Praise God, thank you, Jesus!

Soon, my table and kitchen counters were piled high with groceries—more than we'd ever seen at one time. We were truly learning how to live by faith. To see God supply like that was more than my heart could contain.

Little by little, God taught us the importance of living by faith. I learned with each trial how faith was the key to all God's infinite grace and blessings for those who faithfully follow in his steps. I began to understand the importance of Hebrews 10:35, which says, "Therefore, do not throw away your confidence, which has a great reward." Having confidence in God is believing God will fulfill his promise and knowing he will do what he says. I know prayer works because of my experiences.

15

A Blind Pastor's Wife Trusting God

With Acie's upcoming graduation, school was now behind him. This new milestone thrust us into a time of transition as we sought God for the next step we were to take. We were growing in our marriage, our faith, and our expectations for the future. Acie could now become a candidate for a pastorate. With his master's degree in hand, he would be able to obtain a good position that would fulfill his call and provide for our needs as well.

Two churches extended invitations for him to come preach during the same week as school ended. One of the invitations came from a small church in Louisiana. However, it was only a part-time position. What that actually meant in the ministry was full-time work but not full-time pay. If Acie took that position, he'd also have to take a secular job to supplement his income.

The other church had a considerably larger congregation in Kentucky. This was a full-time pastoral position. This might seem like an easy decision, but we wanted to go where God wanted us and not choose the church based on who paid the most.

Acie and I prayed diligently about the decision. Though it didn't make sense financially, we felt led to take the smaller church.

So, in September we said farewell to our duplex and friends in Tennessee and moved back to Louisiana where Acie became the pastor of Crossroads Baptist Church located about thirty minutes east of Monroe in Farmerville, Louisiana. This wasn't a new area for us as we were now only about forty miles from Bastrop where Acie's parents lived. God brought Acie back close to home.

As Acie stepped into his role as pastor, the two of us worked as a team. Acie did the preaching, teaching, weddings, and funerals, while I took on the role of music director. I also taught a college and career class and organized the missionary circle so we could pray for and meet the needs of the missionaries the church supported. Together, we did community and hospital visitation. Our part-time role was as busy as I'd predicted.

Filling the role of the music director with limited vision had its own challenges and consumed several hours each day. First, I chose the songs each week by listening to recordings. Then I sat at the piano and played until I found which key the song was in and learned the four harmony parts so I could teach them to the choir. I worked hard to have the words and music memorized by mid-week and then presented the song to the choir of twenty-five-to-thirty people at our weekly rehearsal on Wednesday nights. I memorized all the songs the church people loved. Frequently, I pitched in by playing the piano for our Sunday night service, fellowship times, funerals, and other gatherings.

Following the evening service, church people came to our home for a 'singspiration,' which I enjoyed so much. Today they call it a 'hymn-sing.' We sang gospel quartet music everyone loved and could harmonize on songs taken from the Stamp Baxter Gospel Quartet music books rather than from the hymnbook. Even the kids and teenagers joined in. I served finger foods so everyone could help themselves. We used it as a time to get to know each other better and build community within the church.

GOD SAID YES!

In the months that had a fifth Sunday, several churches in the community would come together and share a meal on the church grounds after the morning service, and we'd sing together all afternoon. Everyone participated in singing all the songs with enthusiasm and excitement in four-part harmony. A true anointing filled those gatherings. Music was a vehicle that joined God's people together on a spiritual level, more so than if it were a mere concert group because everyone got to sing and participate and lift their voices to God.

God created us to worship him through singing. He also created us for relationship with himself and with others. These community gatherings provided for that need on both levels and left people feeling filled and satisfied. Though we were busy, the work was fun, fulfilling, and satisfying.

I was thankful my eyes didn't show my blindness. I did my best to hide it when people were around. Even though I loved everything about ministry work, at times I wasn't comfortable in my role as the minister's wife. For instance, I was hesitant to invite guests in for dinner unless I could have everything ready on the table prior to their arrival. Serving buffet style worked best for me, like I did at the singspiration get together. Yet, I was always a little apprehensive, fearing something could go wrong, like a spill that would require my attention. I'd be embarrassed if I had to clean it up in front of people while not being able to see what I was doing. I know it was a silly thought, but I wanted to appear to be as normal as I possibly could.

I prayed every time we entered the church that God would remind me to open my eyes at the close of a prayer. I didn't want to have my eyes closed when everyone else had them open. When one can't see, it's easy to forget to open one's eyes. It's distractive.

Several years had passed since I'd seen myself in the mirror. Life changed me and I had to learn to change with it. Fitting in, dressing properly, using correct gestures, and walking with confidence were important, and yet I had to trust the choices of my hairstyle, makeup, and clothing styles to others. That's scary.

Acie was a tremendous help in this area. He told me if anything was wrong, such as if my slip was showing or if I had a run in my hosiery. He helped me achieve the right hair style and let me know if my makeup needed any adjustment before leaving the house. I also had to trust my friends to tell me if I did anything that was awkward or strange. This need for personal dependence upon others made me feel handicapped. I would've preferred not to have had to depend upon others for these things. But whether I liked it or not, I was handicapped. Friends extended a compliment now and then which assured me all was well, and I appreciated that.

I often felt people were watching me because I was blind. That's normal. People do take notice. I prayed and asked the Lord to help me maintain a healthy emotional attitude, but I constantly struggled with it. I wasn't insecure but simply knew to double check myself.

One time, I overheard Acie talking with someone in our congregation. "Marolyn has been fantastic in the way she's coped with her blindness over the years," he said.

In reality, I didn't think I was handling things that great, but I was encouraged to hear his kind words. He was always thoughtful and knew when to speak a compliment.

I didn't need to know why I was blind. I hadn't done anything to deserve this strange twist of fate, but I learned to trust that in the midst of this, God was at work, taking a bad situation and turning it around for good.

Three specific Scriptures sustained me during those years. "So will My word be which goes forth from My mouth; It will not return to Me empty, Without accomplishing what I desire, And without succeeding in the matter for which I sent it"(Isaiah 55:11).

I also learned healing is given to us in the atonement the same as our salvation. "And by his scourging we are healed" (Isaiah 53:5). Healing is a part of the finished work that Christ accomplished for us on the cross. We are to ask and receive God's gifts by faith. God said, "For as many as are the promises of God, in Him they are yes" (II Corinthians 1:20). I believed God and stood on his Word for my healing. All I had to do was to stay focused on trusting God, my healer.

I clung to these Scriptures. They were my hope and the anchor of my faith. The Bible was certainly my source of comfort and strength as I stood by faith on God's Words of promise. I'd never heard of miracles taking place on earth other than in the Bible days, and these promises gave me great peace in the midst of my storm.

I always wondered how people who didn't rely upon God made it through their storms in life. They had no hope to cling to. In the midst of my struggle, I had my Jesus. He became my friend, my constant source of strength.

Yes, I was blind, but victory was mine because Jesus came to set the captives free. I didn't have to live in defeat or in bondage to my physical limitation. To focus on what I didn't have invited unhappiness and misery. To focus on Jesus, the author and finisher of my faith, established an inner joy and peace. God longed for intimacy with me, as he does with all his children.

I had victory of spirit in the midst of living with this handicap, which encouraged others who were going through hardships in life.

16

A Courageous Decision

Over the years, my vision deteriorated so severely that if someone waved their hand directly in front of my nose, I could only make out shadows. But I never gave up hope. Whether through medications or an eye transplant, I somehow felt I would see again. I had to believe the Scripture verse that says, "Now faith is the assurance of *things* hoped for, the conviction of things not seen" (Hebrews 11:1). I needed this kind of substance as a solid foundation to stand on.

After moving to north Louisiana, my new doctor recommended I attend the State Rehabilitation for the Blind in Little Rock, Arkansas, for training. With Acie's education behind us, I decided to further my education.

Acie was the pastor of a bivocational church and worked in a men's clothing store to supplement our income. So, our biggest concern was who would have the time to take care of Sharon while I was away for three months.

My parents couldn't keep her because they were in Michigan, and we felt she needed to stay somewhat close to Acie so he could at least see her once a week after work.

After much prayer and discussion, God worked it out for Acie's parents to have Sharon during the weekdays. Although they were both employed, Acie's dad covered shift work.

"We can make the schedule work," they told us. "Sharon can stay with us and attend daycare."

It became clear to us why the Lord had led us to accept the pastorate position of the smaller church in Louisiana rather than the larger church in Kentucky. God had looked ahead into the future and provided.

After several months of completing the paperwork to enroll in the Arkansas Enterprise for the Adult Blind, the day finally arrived for Acie and Sharon to take me to Little Rock, Arkansas, for my training.

I would now be learning new skills I could bring back home to create some new kind of normal, hopefully.

The school curriculum was set up so each student could progress at their own speed. That meant if I worked hard, I could get back home to Acie and Sharon as soon as possible—a frightening comfort. I was determined to push myself to the limit, work with diligence, and learn quickly in unfamiliar surroundings. I had to picture in my mind's eye the layout of buildings on the school campus. I couldn't see steps, people, walls, or furniture.

I'd grown accustomed to Acie's skilled verbal instruction and guidance to help me maneuver in new areas, but at school I was on my own.

Once again, I was forced to rely on strangers for physical and emotional support I needed to complete this program. The thought made me shudder. I soon learned to appreciate the caring instruction and guidance from the staff who were trained to work with the blind and who could teach me skills to help me cope and interact with people more productively.

I needed to learn things we take for granted in a sighted world. For an example, one time when Sharon was young, we were visiting in the home of one of our church members. She and her husband had just built and furnished a beautiful home. Our hostess served coffee and cake and placed Sharon's glass of iced tea and cake on the end table beside the sofa where Sharon was seated. Although I couldn't see the situation, I realized my daughter was going to have to reach over the armrest to pick up her glass of tea or to eat her cake. Concerned for the new sofa and surroundings, I felt there was less chance for an accident of spilling if Sharon were seated at the coffee table in front of us. As I reached to move the tea glass, I inadvertently bumped the edge and sent the tea spilling over the sofa, creating the accident I'd hoped to avoid. Thank goodness for Herculean fabric; I'm told it never left a spot. But the incident revealed how badly I needed to attend the school for the blind. The blind could learn to touch a glass without causing a spill, though I'd miss my family while gone to school.

17

WHEN RUNNING AWAY ISN'T AN OPTION

Leaving me at the School for the Adult Blind was incredibly hard for all three of us. Being my protector, Acie panicked at the thought of me being alone in that strange place and was the most difficult thing he ever had to do. In our ten years of marriage, he and I hadn't been apart—not even for one night. The thought of being separated for an extended period of time was almost unbearable for me.

Acie helped check me in and get my belongings situated in my room. We both shed tears while saying goodbye as he and my three-year-old daughter got in the car for the trip back. They were going home, and I was staying in a cold, dark dorm room.

After they left, a hollow, empty feeling settled in the pit of my stomach. Although there were people all around me, I felt so alone. And I didn't even know where the walls, doors, or furniture were located. I tried hard not to feel sorry for myself.

Then I heard the Holy Spirit whisper, "Do not fear, for I am with you; do not anxiously look about you, for I am your God. I will strengthen you, surely I will help you. Surely I will uphold you with my righteous right hand" (Isaiah 41:10). Did I really believe that? Yes. Those words carried me through the difficult weeks ahead as the time of separation became more and more difficult.

Acie and I spent many hours on the phone crying.

My heart would break as little Sharon would cry, "Mommy, when will you come home? I miss you Mommy." At the point of despair, Isaiah 41:10 became my lifeline.

Classes started immediately, and I was thrust into the new environment and program that would teach me how to function sightless in a sighted world. One either adjusted or got left behind. I'm sure this was done for a reason so participants didn't have time to change their minds and run home.

In addition to practical training, the school required the trainees attend a therapy class. Since I was new, I was asked to introduce myself and share my feelings regarding my total loss of vision. Never before had I expressed those feelings to anyone. I was the girl who was petrified to talk with my classmates and teacher in the small, two-room schoolhouse when I was in elementary school, and here the instructor asked me to bare my soul before a group of complete strangers who I couldn't even see. Not a chance.

I played it safe and shared about my concern for Sharon and her inability to understand my absence.

The instructor listened patiently, then digging deeper, asked, "Marolyn, is there anything else bothering you that you might want to talk about today?"

His compassion was genuine, but I was too uncomfortable to open up my heart to people I didn't know. I had no idea who I was talking to. Nausea swept over me and in a panic, I ran away from the group to my room and crashed upon my bed. Overwhelmed at having left the security of home with its familiar surroundings and Acie at my side helping me, I was inundated with homesickness and a flood of emotions, and I wept. Thank goodness nobody came running after me. They must have known I needed time alone. Eventually, I regained my composure and made my way back to the group. I still wasn't ready to share but sat listening and completed that session. Maybe I could do this, and by God's power, I would.

Had it not been for one instructor, John Strickland, I might not have made it through. Mr. Strickland happened to be sitting in on the therapy class that first day, listening, and taking notes for another man in the session who was deaf and blind. Mr. Strickland later became my mobility (white cane) instructor, but that afternoon, when I was brand new to the program and knew no one, he took the time to come talk with me after the class was dismissed. He spoke with compassion and seemed to know exactly what I was feeling inside.

I learned that he too had been blind for a period of three years before surgery corrected his visual problem. Unfortunately, for me, surgery wasn't an option. I was blind, and as the good doctor at the Mayo Clinic had said, I had to learn to live with it.

But that afternoon, as Mr. Strickland and I sat across from each other, he came right to the point and helped me understand that my emotional stress stemmed from the fact I was a normal person who happened to be blind and was experiencing an abnormal situation. In essence, he helped me to understand my response was perfectly normal.

I needed to hear him say that, and his words of affirmation brought me great comfort. The loss of what little bit of vision I had severely affected me emotionally. I don't think I realized how much until he brought it to my attention so vividly. He made me draw it to the surface of my mind and face it—something I didn't want to do. I was learning to deal with the emotional and physical limitations of blindness more realistically.

That afternoon, thanks to Mr. Strickland and the other instructors I'd meet over the next several days, I started on a path to adjust to my life of gaining useful life skills.

Over the next few days, an instructor walked beside me, showing me where each building and classroom was located.

About one week into my training, I was given a new permanent accessory to my life—a personalized long, slender, white Hoover cane. This became an extension of my sense of touch so I could regain my independence. First, I was taught how to hold it correctly and become familiar with its feel. The next step was to learn to use the cane using short strokes with a side-to-side motion no wider or further apart than my feet were when walking. This helped me to locate obstacles in my pathway, like doors, steps, and turns.

I learned how to determine where the outside entrances to the buildings were located. Each building had a sidewalk with a slight elevation that leveled off when approaching the entrance doors. Then they slanted back down to normal level after passing the entrance. Once familiar with this instruction and similar tips given in the brief walk-through orientation, I was expected to make my way around campus on my own. I was definitely nervous and hoped I wouldn't get lost or run into anyone.

The training center and staff were extremely organized and had a set procedure for everything. When we went to the dining hall to eat, we were to leave our white canes hanging on a coat rack at the bottom of the staircase, go up the stairs, and follow a three-foot-wide strip of carpet around the edge of the room which served as a path to guide us to the buffet counter.

The kitchen staff would set our plates on the counter in front of us. They knew that if they tried to hand a plate to us, we could miss it and cause a spill. Everything we did trained us for successful outcomes in life.

After getting our food, we would then go to the tables. With my plate in my left hand, I felt for the tables with my right. We were assigned to a specific table, so I counted tables until I came to the row where my table sat. One. Two. Three. Unfortunately, not everyone used this same method. Some trainees were so afraid of spilling food they'd clutch their plate with both hands and would steer themselves with the plate out front rather than guiding themselves with one free hand. I thought they would be more likely to spill their food moving in this manner, but each of us had to learn to maneuver in our own way. While locating our assigned tables, often someone crashed a plate into the back of my head and spilled food on me. Patience and understanding were virtues we each needed to receive and extend to those around us.

We didn't have a choice regarding who would sit at what table or with whom we would eat our meals. I was assigned a specific chair at a table that would seat four. We were instructed that this was to be our same seat for the duration of the training.

Meals, like everything else, were an exercise in patience. I had to familiarize myself with the table set up. The napkin holder was placed in the middle of the table with the salt and pepper located on the far side of the napkin container from where I sat. The butter was to the right of the napkins and the sugar, on the left. Thankfully, the table was set up the same for every meal. That never changed.

My table partners were three men. One really annoyed me. Frequently, when he reached for the sugar, his fingers landed in my dessert. Licking his finger with a loud smack of his lips, he apologized each time after the mishap. I could have excused it more easily if he'd followed the correct procedure our instructors taught us, which was to glide our hand around the items on the table to locate what was needed, rather than reaching up and over. I never treated this man with disrespect, but the temptation was there. I guess because God's people were praying for me, I was given the grace to hold back … barely.

One day, after he left the table, I asked the dining help if we could switch the placement of the sugar on our table so he could find it without reaching over the napkins and landing in my dessert. They accommodated my request, but unfortunately, it didn't solve the problem. He usually forgot and reached across the napkins and landed in my dessert anyway.

After exiting the dining room, I could easily locate which cane was mine among the many hanging on the coat rack hooks at the bottom of the staircase. Each cane had been tailored to fit our height. If I made an error and accidentally grabbed someone else's cane, it didn't feel right. After a short time, my cane became as familiar to me as Acie's voice. We'd been instructed to place a distinctive trinket at the top of the cane where a chain hung for that purpose.

Still, sometimes someone would pick up the wrong cane—mine. I knew not to borrow another cane hanging there because then someone else would be stranded. Instead, I had to wait at the coat rack until either the person realized they had the wrong cane and brought it back or I could catch the arm of someone going to my dorm and tag alone with them.

Eventually, whoever had my cane would return it to the coat rack, often when they came to the dining room for the next meal. Being at the mercy of someone else's carelessness wasn't easy. It rubbed against my independent nature. Whether I liked it or not, God used these small challenges to shape and mold me into a more patient and kinder individual as I continued to adjust in this sightless world.

18

WE DON'T GROW IN OUR COMFORT ZONE

Contrary to popular belief, the loss of one of our senses doesn't necessarily cause our other senses to automatically compensate. My sense of touch, hearing, smell, and taste needed to sharpen, but that would only come through concentration and training, not simply as a natural result of loss. Developing these skills drained me both mentally and physically.

I discovered how much I much took for granted—all the things sight allows us to process. For example, when paying for an item, the sighted could easily distinguish the difference in paper money. But even with our coins, although they come in different sizes, we use our sight to double check whether we grabbed a dime or a penny.

When we hear water come to a boil, we use sight to verify bubbles and the intensity of the boil. Yet, the blind are totally dependent on other senses to make these assessments. So, by default, other senses do increase but only through hard work and out of necessity.

Eventually, I learned how to make these determinations using my other senses until it became second nature and didn't require all my concentration. Finally, as I gained trust in my sense of perception, I was able to believe I could live a more normal existence.

One day, while my instructor and I were talking, I smelled heat. I knew he didn't smoke, and it didn't smell like cigarettes. When he finished talking, I asked him if he smelled heat. He said he held a lit cigarette lighter about six inches in front of my face. I couldn't see the light, but I could feel the effect of the flame.

"What was the purpose?" I asked, rather perplexed.

"I wanted to check your ability to perceive light," he informed me.

Unfortunately, I failed that test completely.

Learning how to use the white cane and walk in a straight line wasn't easy or fun. I first had to get over my embarrassment of carrying the cane in public. Of course, it didn't bother me while at the Training Center where everyone carried a cane but using it around sighted people while in training on the streets in Little Rock made me feel as if everyone was watching me.

My practice ground was the city sidewalk. The instructor would take us to this public venue to practice. I soon learned that if I veered too much to the right or left, it could be dangerous as well as confusing to anyone coming in front or behind me. At first, I must have looked like I was drunk because I was all over the sidewalk. I couldn't walk in a straight line down the middle of the walkway. I kept veering over too far, touching the grass on the right and then a little further down I moved too far to the left and touched the grass on that side.

My instructor informed me that holding the cane in the right position had a lot to do with the success of being able to walk in a straight line. The cane must be held correctly. After a couple weeks of practice, I walked down the middle of the sidewalk without using the grass as my guideline. Another major victory.

Over time, I became dependent upon the cane and its usefulness in my life. From then on, I used it unashamedly.

Back at the blind school, surprisingly, the things which frightened me most were stairways. Going up was a challenge; going down was even worse. I felt as though I was going to fall forward on my face and grabbed hold of the rail and hung on as I placed one foot on the step followed by the other until both feet were securely on the step before progressing to the next—a pitiful, slow process. To make a difficult situation even worse, stairs and steps were all over that campus. If sighted people are blindfolded, most are able to go up and down stairs without any trouble. But the blind can't without practice to regain their confidence in motor memory.

After a couple weeks of my slow progress, Mr. Strickland asked, "When are you going to start walking those steps like you used to do?"

"What do you mean?" I asked, even though I knew what he meant.

"Before you were blind, when you were back in high school, you didn't put two feet on one step and pause before you went down the stairs, did you? You put a foot on each step and kept going. Don't be afraid," he encouraged me.

Right then, I realized what I was doing and quickly determined no matter how insecure I felt, I'd work at regaining my motor skill memory and master those steps.

Two other skills taught at the school for the blind were typing and spelling. I already knew how to type, so that was no problem. I'd always been good at spelling and often won the spelling bees. I wanted to make the best use of my time while attending the Training Center for the Blind and felt I'd already mastered this skill of spelling, so when they were scheduling my classes, I opted out of the spelling class.

"How long have you been blind?" the class instructor asked in response to my request.

"Since I was eighteen," I replied.

"Anyone who's been blind for that long has lost much of their ability to spell because of not having been able to see the printed page. Let's take the test and see how you do."

I took the test and much to my chagrin, I failed. I couldn't believe spelling was a skill I lost. Without hesitation, I immediately enrolled in the refresher spelling course.

Both male and female alike were required to learn how to do wood crafts in shop class, which included using the electric tools like a saw and sander ... yes, without sight. The wood crafts, along with knitting and crocheting, were to develop sensitivity in our fingers and to develop our sense of touch for reading Braille dots and practical living. I was amazed at how the practical application of these classes achieved their intended result.

Crocheting was no problem, so I decided I'd make a child's sweater during the course.

But the wood craft portion was another story. I had to get over my fear of using the electrical equipment. Although rather scary, I quickly saw the importance of these classes and skills. I grew to trust the instructors who were helping me learn skills to achieve a new level of independence in life.

Learning Braille was one of the more difficult challenges I faced. Braille is made up of six little raised dots. When arranged in different positions they form every word, punctuation mark, number, Roman numeral, fraction, and decimal point used in the English language. An amazing system—all from six little dots.

When I was learning the alphabet and simple words, the lessons were easy, and I could move forward quickly. But the alphabet letters in themselves were not used to spell out an entire word. Braille was like shorthand. The same two dots that stand for the letter "K" also stand for the word *know* or *knowledge*, depending on which dots precede the "K" dots.

"M" stood for the word *more*, but a dot five, before the "M" meant it stood for *mother*. These same dots or alphabet letters used with different dots preceding them, would stand for many different words—an exercise in memorization and practice, pure and simple.

Suddenly, the day came when I couldn't comprehend any more of the lessons in Braille. I'd been progressing at a quick pace, but now, my ability to learn came to a standstill.

Oh, dear, that's all I can learn. I became frustrated and discouraged, as I knew I had much more to learn. Fortunately, my instructor was able to put my heart to rest.

"Marolyn, you'll be fine," he encouraged. "You're trying to comprehend too much too fast. Take a break for a few days, absorb and practice what you already learned. Then come back, and you'll be able to progress forward."

Sure enough, after a few days, I returned to class and my progress continued as before. I breathed a sigh of relief, knowing that even in these small areas, God was in control. He never left me, his child, without the assistance I needed.

"You either have to laugh or cry," the old adage says. I had plenty of opportunities to do both during my three-month tenure at the School for the Blind.

I recall one incident shortly after learning to use the white cane. My mobility instructor took me downtown Little Rock for an exercise in public so I could practice my ability to be able to maneuver successfully around people, places, and things. He gave me a specific route to follow while another trainee had the same route, only in reverse. This meant, at some point our paths would meet.

Unfortunately, the other trainee hadn't yet learned a white cane was a delicate instrument intended to be tapped in short strides lightly from side to side.

The young man was quite robust in his tapping skill. I heard him coming, slapping his cane from far right to far left as though trying to tear the sidewalk apart.

Whap! Whap! Whap!

At that same time, I walked in front of a bus stop as three noisy buses drove up to the curb. The racket of the buses drowned out all other sounds, so I could no longer hear the slapping of this other guy's cane.

I slowed my gait to avoid a possible collision. Because of the location and all the people around me waiting to catch a bus, I wouldn't be able to make any sudden move to the right or to the left. Unsure of my position. I simply stopped and stood still until the buses moved on.

The trainee had to be coming closer. Unsure how to proceed, I decided to call out, but my voice was drowned out by all the din from all the busses.

Then all of a sudden, *Whap! Whap! Whap!* The blind man collided with me, knocking both of us to the ground. We must have been a sight with our arms, legs, and canes tossing around and tangled up in each other.

"Marolyn, is that you?" he called out. Although not funny at the time, later I could chuckle over the spectacle we caused. Being the brunt of the entertainment was one event I hoped to avoid in the future.

GOD SAID YES!

I often went with a group from the Training Center on short day trips. One was to tour an old homestead. I remember the guide standing only four feet in front of us, but through the entire tour, he shouted at the top of his voice. Often, individuals would raise their voice when speaking with us as though we couldn't hear because we couldn't see. This happened more frequently than one might expect.

Although it would have been easy to become irritated with him, we overlooked it. I chuckle at it now. I knew he meant well.

Another time, I was in the lobby at the bottom of the stairs that went up to the dining room, talking with another trainee who I'll name "Tommy." Although he was diagnosed as legally blind, he had some visual capacity. As we stood and talked, another female friend walked in.

Unlike Tommy, she had no visibility. Upon entering the lobby and making her way over to the steps, she slightly brushed against the coke machine. "Oh, excuse me!" she apologized in a sweet, humble manner. "I didn't mean to bump into you." No one was in the lobby but us.

Tommy could see well enough to realize what happened. He couldn't contain his laughter as she apologized to the inanimate object. We all had a good laugh together. Yes, life as a blind person provided continual opportunities to laugh at our mistakes and learn not to take ourselves so seriously. But that's good advice for everyone.

A joyful heart is good medicine, But a broken spirit dries up the bones (Proverbs 17:22).

19

POWER IN WEAKNESS

Although the driving distance between our home in Louisiana and the training center in Little Rock, Arkansas, was only a six-hour trip, the physical and emotional distance it put between me and my family made it seem as if I were halfway around the world.

Acie and Sharon experienced some difficulties to come visit during the three months I was at the training center. Acie had to ask off work on Saturday once a month in order to come. The loss of revenue from that workday, plus the added expense for gas and travel, stretched our already-strained budget. His schedule was already a challenge without these trips. He and Sharon drove over on Saturday morning a hundred fifty miles to spend a few hours with me. Then, he had to drive back that evening and be ready to preach on Sunday.

Physical distance was only one challenge in the equation. Each time Acie and Sharon visited, I noted a marked 'cultural distance.' He had difficulty relating to my new friends who were all blind. It's one thing to be required to interact with an entire group of strangers but add the blindness factor into the scenario, and whether we want to admit it or not, it complicates the exchange.

No matter what the disability, others can become uncomfortable if they aren't accustomed to overlooking the obvious. In my case, blindness. It doesn't change the fact that the person inside the physically limited body is not only able but desires to communicate and have normal relationships.

Acie was never able to get over the feeling of being out of place at the Blind Center, and I could understand how he felt. I would've felt that same awkwardness if I were in his shoes. Thankfully, my mobility instructor was instrumental in bridging this gap. Since he lived in both worlds and had since regained his sight through surgery, he had a unique perspective and ability to relate to both sides of the spectrum. He became a tremendous help, and we relied on his council and assistance over and over during that season of life.

Sharon was another story. The separation anxiety she felt each time they left after a visit with her mama was heart-wrenching. While she understood I was there because I needed to learn how to do things that would help me in my work, the longer I was away, the harder it was on her. She wanted things back to normal too. She wanted us all back together under one roof and to live with her parents again. She loved her grandparents, but she became homesick and cried inconsolably each time they left for home without me and every time Acie had to leave her behind to spend another week in Bastrop away from home.

I thought of my insecurity when the high school principal separated my sister Carolyn and me all day long, every day, when we'd never been separated before. That wasn't anything compared to Sharon having to be separated from her love and security of home at such a young age. I prayed every day she wouldn't feel insecure and wouldn't think I wasn't coming back or that her daddy and I didn't love her or each other.

The weekends they didn't come to visit were no less stressful on Acie. He worked six days a week—Monday through Saturday—at his job as a clothing salesman. Immediately after work on Saturday, he would drive thirty miles to pick up Sharon from his parents in Bastrop, Louisiana, and bring her another forty-five-minute drive back home to Farmerville, Louisiana, to spend a little time with him in her familiar surroundings. And he had to be ready to preach two services on Sunday. Then after preaching on Sunday evening, he drove Sharon back to his parents' in Bastrop for another week. Those three months were difficult for all.

I learned later that every time Acie had to drop her off with his parents on Sunday night, Sharon cried and cried and wouldn't let go of him, begging him … pleading with him … to take her home and not leave without her.

Our temporary separation was hard on Acie's parents too. They had to pry her little arms away from her daddy and hold her sobbing in their arms as Acie went out the door and left for home, leaving her behind. Every week that passed became more difficult. Not only was Sharon homesick, but Acie felt like he too couldn't keep this schedule for much longer.

Many people don't realize the strain on the rest of the family relationships when one family member has a disability. Everyone is affected. Everyone must adjust during this season. Acie carried a huge burden—much greater than people realized. As a pastor, one who was expected to be the leader and encourager for his congregation, he struggled. The emotional and physical stress we experienced as a family left him with little to give back to his congregation.

The three months I was at school seemed like a year. The last month became unbearable for all of us. I was obligated to stay to the finish.

Acie simply couldn't take being separated any longer. To stand in the pulpit, face the people, and preach another sermon with the burden of our being apart resting upon him became too much for him as well. We were all being stretched to the limit physically and emotionally. We were taking hold of God and barely holding on.

Over the phone every Saturday night, I tried to encourage him and lift his spirit for the Sunday meetings. During that difficult time, Acie said the Lord gave him this verse. "My grace is sufficient for you, for power is perfected in weakness" (II Corinthians 12:9). He found great strength in those words and quoted them to me every Saturday night in tears of deep anguish before we hung up the phone. Both our hearts were ripping as we cried together. Cell phones hadn't been invented yet, and long distant calls were expensive, so we limited our calls to once a week.

My goal was to complete my training in three months rather than in six in order to get back to my family. I divided up my Braille lessons into three sections, hoping I could learn the entire set each month and not get behind schedule. The task was almost impossible, but I kept reminding myself I needed to finish and get my family back together.

I had one month to go. It looked like I would reach my goal to complete the training in only three months. Yet, it felt like a lifetime stretched before us until we'd be reunited. That goal drove me to push harder than I could ever remember being stretched. I needed to get back to Acie and Sharon before they reached the breaking point—or I did.

20

Going Home—Facing Life with Courage

Acie and Sharon came to bring me home. I'd met my goal. Mr. Strickland was extremely encouraging as I prepared to leave. He commented to Acie regarding my ability to learn Braille in such a short amount of time. I couldn't have done it without God helping me. Three months had seemed like forever, but the life skills I learned would serve me well in the years that followed. Nothing could top how good it felt to be going home with my little family.

Acie was amazed when he saw all the practical things I learned. I could finally put that new training to good use. He had to get used to the cane, though. After returning home from the School for the Adult Blind, he and I were getting out of the car to go shopping.

"Just leave your cane in the car," he commented.

This would be Acie's first time with me while using my cane in public and around people we knew. So, I understood his comment. I'd always taken his arm, and by walking one half-step behind him, he guided me through each situation. With the cane, I was more independent, though my sight was gone completely. People who knew me knew that I couldn't see, but others didn't. My eyes didn't show they were blind.

People knew I had limited vision, but using the cane publicly announced to the world that I now was blind. At the beginning,

I was embarrassed to be seen in public using the cane. Now, I needed to help Acie feel comfortable in making this public adjustment.

That may sound prideful to some, but I called it "human." We're all human, and we have to learn to adjust to things, especially when it's on public display. However, before long, Acie became comfortable when he realized how much I benefited from its use. He also saw how differently people treated me—in a helpful way—when I carried it and how difficult it was for me to be without it. Yes, the cane had become our new friend.

I stepped back into my position as mom and pastor's wife, picking up where I had left off, teaching my young adult Sunday school class and working with the choir and the Women's Missionary Society, only now with more skill.

Acie no longer had to accompany me everywhere. With my new skills, I moved around easier and safer on my own. For example, I did a lot of church visitation and needed landmarks along the way. I could find my way to the local community grocery store near our home and the church by leaving the parsonage on the church property, walking over to the side of the church building and around to the front entrance to establish focal points.

From there, I was able to locate the church sign, which was my next landmark, and after that I followed the roadside grass to the corner where two highways intersected. I could judge how far I'd progressed by listening to the traffic sounds, which also helped me determine when safe to cross the highway. The community store was located on the corner where the two highways met. Once on the store parking lot, I discovered another marker where the pavement had been torn up making a gravel path to the store.

GOD SAID YES!

Our church was located in a rural community. Part of my ministry was to visit the church members who were sick as well as the elderly and those who had missed church regularly. I could make these home visits without assistance. I walked along the lawns on the edge of the road, and when my cane hit gravel, I knew I'd reached a driveway. All I had to do was count the correct number of driveways in order to visit the right house or listen for a dog in the back yard.

Dogs also became landmarks for me. They always barked at my approach, and I soon recognized their distinctive barks and knew where they lived. All of these became road signs for me to successfully get to my destination. Because the community was so small, I could visit everyone who was within walking distance of the church parsonage.

At times, when I went out to visit our church parishioners, feelings of insecurity rose up and threatened to overwhelm me. One day, as I walked along the roadside, my cane suddenly hit a parked car. I nearly jumped out of my skin. My mind had been on other things, and I hadn't been as acutely aware of my surroundings as I should've been. While it may sound like 'no big deal' to a sighted individual, the parked car completely shook me to the core. It caught me off guard. Sometimes these unexpected encounters caused enormous frustration, but they were good reminders for me to stay focused at all times.

On one of my excursions, I encountered a barking, growling dog advancing toward me. I became greatly relieved when suddenly, he came to a standstill within three feet of me. I later learned the animal was inside a fenced yard. My heart still raced each time I walked past him.

Without sight, small things became big things. As a blind person, I required more motivation to venture out because of these unknown dangers. Whether a broken sidewalk, holes in the ground or pavement, rocks, hills, thick grass, tree twigs, or a dog, stepping out on my own was never easy. However, I had enough confidence not to let that keep me from going out to do the work of the Lord.

I was forever learning, and my learning process became Sharon's as well. As a preschooler, she needed to learn how to cross streets safely, just as I did. So, we helped each other. These became training sessions for both of us as I taught her not only to use her sight, but also her hearing and other indicators to determine if it was safe to cross the road.

When I returned from getting the mail out of the mailbox, the first question Sharon asked as I walked back into the house was, "Mama, were you careful when you crossed that highway?"

A little role reversal to be sure, but her increased awareness of traffic dangers due to my situation became a good habit for her own safety. When Sharon was in elementary school, people often commented on how careful she was when crossing the streets as she walked to and from school. Although she carried a sense of responsibility, I wish she wouldn't have had to shoulder my well-being.

Still, at the same time, we became stronger through this challenge. The difficulties we encountered during those years grew all of us in different ways. I watched Sharon grow in her ability to be considerate, caring, cautious—in good ways—and observant, due to the unique situation in our home with my blindness. I recognized how God used the Scripture verse, "And we know that God causes all things to work together for good to those who love God" (Romans 8:28) in taking our difficult situation to develop skills, character, and a deep sense of compassion in my daughter.

How wonderfully freeing to be able to be out on church visitation on my own while Acie was working. Slowly, I began to feel as if my life again had more purpose and meaning. My labor of love ministered as much to me as it did to those I visited.

Obviously, my sense of hearing had become extremely important to me. Simple things became indicators that replaced normal visual markers. For example, when uncooked chicken is placed in the hot skillet to brown, it's noisy, but as the meat becomes tender the sizzling dies away. This was my indicator to set a timer and turn the heat to a low simmer. That's what gives fried chicken its flavor.

I listened for the changes in sound as I poured a beverage. As the liquid neared the rim, the sound changed and let me know when to stop pouring.

Sounds became markers and indicators to navigate around a room. It's easy for a blind person to become completely disoriented even in familiar surroundings. I learned to listen to the sounds around me, pausing to listen for a refrigerator in the kitchen, or the tick-tock of a clock in the bedroom. Things that made noise that stayed in the same location day after day were indicators as to which way I was facing in a room. Pushing myself for three months while learning how to develop these senses at the blind school was one of the best things I'd done for myself, although I hated the family separation because it had taken such a toll on all of us.

My cane had become one of my most important assets. Walking anywhere, whether in the city, country or at conference meetings obviously held many challenges. I needed to listen for unexpected sounds above all the clamor around me. I paid attention to the change in sound as I tapped my cane on the sidewalk which indicated I was on an incline or on a decline. Small concrete squares produced a different sound than larger ones. Tapping in front of a brick building makes a sound different than in front of a glass-fronted building. The sound of traffic, squealing brakes, whistles blowing, and roaring thunder were all critical warning signals that helped guide me, keep me safe, and know where I was on my journey.

While walking by store fronts, I noticed the odors coming from inside. Each shop had a unique aroma that wafted from its walls: the coffee shop, bakery, convenience store with tobacco, peanuts, and popcorn. I could recognize the bank with its distinct aroma of money. When in a department store, the odors pointed me to the cosmetic counter with its variety of perfumes, or the shoe department with the smell of leather, or the kitchen baking aisle with its blend of spices and seasonings. These smells became as familiar to me as a sign does to the sighted consumer.

In addition to my growing confidence and daily practices, I also was able to be independent in our daily business affairs. With the loss of sight, things which once were simple, like paying a bill and writing a check, were no longer so straightforward. Yet they were necessary. Thankfully, after learning Braille and some other skills, such as how to use an abacus and a check-writing template, I was well on my way to regaining independence in these areas as well.

Another unique trick enabled me to hand write letters to people even though I couldn't see the paper or the end result. Using a board with strings tacked in place horizontally from right to left to indicate lines on the page, I could insert my paper beneath the strings on the board which also held it in place. The strings then became my guides so I could write in straight lines. Already a typist prior to becoming blind, I could still use a keyboard for business letter writing. I didn't like sending them without someone proofing them first since I was unable to see if I made a typo.

In years past, the blind were taught how to write the Braille letters backward from right to left by punching the dots onto a sheet of paper using a slate and stylus then turning the page over and reading the letters from left to right. Braille enabled me to make notes to myself and write down appointments, prescriptions, telephone numbers, recipes, and pretty much everything I needed to keep track of. I also used it to label my spices and seasonings in my kitchen cabinets and some of my canned goods. I didn't have to label all my canned goods. A simple shake would often reveal the contents as I became accustomed to utilizing my other senses.

As always, Acie was still my hero offering to be my eyes. For example, when we went out to eat, he would instruct me as to what was on my plate in terms of a clock. Once the waitress placed my food before me, he would quietly inform me as to what was on my plate and where it was located. This saved me the embarrassment and need to finger my food to locate what was before me, or from putting my fork into my plate and having it come up empty.

Still, even with his assistance pertaining to what was on my plate, some foods gave me a good deal of trouble. Jell-O, for example, was so light I couldn't tell whether it was on the fork or not. A more embarrassing scenario occurred when I thought I had a small piece of meat on my fork only to find out the hard way that it was a big piece.

Usually, when in public, I ordered fish because it separated easily. Eating steak was dangerous. It's so easy for steak to fly off the plate while cutting it. However, when in a restaurant, I could ask to have the cook cut the meat into small pieces before serving it to me. Buttering bread could be a task if the butter was at room temperature. The knife could go right through soft butter without knowing it until it landed on my knuckles. But I liked the butter too much to give it up, so I kept trying.

It's natural for sighted people to close their eyes and open them once the prayer concludes. Not so for a blind person. As simple as it sounds, when you can't see it's easy to forget to open them. So, I made it my prayer and asked the Lord to remind me to open my eyes at the close of every prayer, especially when sitting in church.

It didn't happen overnight, but eventually a day came where I felt "comfortable" with the new me. Friends knew I couldn't see, and they embraced me with their love and friendship. We had truly reached a new level of breakthrough when friends began to joke about my white cane. Not in a "make fun" sort of way, but in a feeling of camaraderie in which I knew they felt comfortable with me.

21

Taking Care of My Daughter

My daughter was probably my biggest motivation to figure out ways to do things. Yet to do the tasks of a normal mother required creativity. Sharon was going on three and needed someone to read to her, so I ordered children's ABC books, Bible stories books, and others that had Braille dots on the left page and printed words with pictures on the right. That way, either Acie or I could read to her. This activity brought such joy as I was able to read to Sharon, but I discovered it also helped me gain speed in reading Braille.

Since I couldn't see, I had to know where Sharon was every minute. I learned to do this by what Sharon called "play work." I invited her to help me with whatever household chore I was doing. When it was time to wash dishes, I pulled a chair up to the sink, wrapped an apron around her and stood her on the chair to help. I gave her unbreakable dishes to wash while I washed all others. Not only did I know where Sharon was, but she learned from an early age how to do simple household tasks. She learned a good work ethic and skills that would serve her well as she grew older.

One doesn't have to see dirt to know it's there. As in any household, things needed to be cleaned. Whenever I mopped or swept the floors, I found it important to do this in a set pattern. I started at one end of the room with a two-foot sweep and followed it across the floor horizontally, then came back and cleaned it again vertically moving across the floor until I had completed the work. I'd miss a spot if I cleaned in a circular pattern.

Also, I let Sharon have her own little mop and water bucket. She became "Mama's little helper." Because she was young, there were some aspects she couldn't imitate in the process. Initially, her hand muscles couldn't ring out the water from her small mop; therefore, all the water landed on the floor. In order to deal with the excess water, I worked barefoot and kept her working ahead of me. My feet could then locate the puddles of water where she had worked on the floor and I could mop it dry. I didn't expect Sharon to actually clean the floors. But by working with me on whatever project I was doing and having her at my side, I knew she wasn't in any danger.

Growing up, Sharon knew not to play on the floor unless she had permission from me. Otherwise, I might accidentally trip over her or the toys. Also, she understood the importance of putting her clothes in the laundry basket when she changed each day, avoiding the possibility that I might stumble over them and hurt her or myself.

She kept a good attitude about these things, even though I could've become frustrated. I always appreciated that about her and thanked God for my sweet daughter. It's important for me to note here that I was careful to make sure Sharon never felt like she had to take on responsibilities beyond her age. That's not healthy. Her helping me was my way of knowing where she was. I always tried to make it fun.

We were a happy family, immersed in the Lord's work, living by his daily grace yet praying continuously for years for divine healing. After all, the Bible says, "And by his scourging we are healed" (Isaiah 53:5). I figured that included me.

22

These Blind Eyes See!

Even with all the progress I'd made, life as a blind person was downright difficult and took a toll on all of us. Add to that the stress on Acie while holding down a secular job and doing church ministry. After working a full day, he'd come home for a quick bite to eat and head right back out to visit those in the hospital, or support the church family through board meetings, wedding rehearsals, and a multitude of other ministering opportunities. Besides that, he had the additional responsibility of some tasks wives normally handled.

We were actually both highly stressed trying to keep up with the ministry work. I had to study and prepare for teaching my college and career Sunday school class. I spent two hours each afternoon visiting parishioners and two hours every morning working on new church music, learning the words and the individual singing parts to teach the choir weekly—time consuming and difficult for me as a blind person. Also, taking care of the household duties and caring for our little girl took twice as much time. How much longer could we keep up this pace?

On the night of August 25, 1972, we drove to Acie's parents to celebrate his birthday with ice cream, cake, and coffee. Saying goodbye around eleven o'clock at night., Sharon begged to stay the night with her grandparents. Acie looked at his mom for approval to make sure they were up to the unexpected request, and they agreed she could stay. Sharon was ecstatic.

Driving home that night, exhausted, Acie and I did some serious talking. Our lives were at a crossroads. Something had to change. But what? We'd been praying about relocating to another church where Acie could be a full-time pastor, but nothing opened up. I knew Acie needed my help, but I felt more like a burden than a helpmate.

I often pleaded, "Oh God, please give sight to my blind eyes. There's so much I need to do, and everything takes twice as long. God I need my eyesight." I never gave up hope that I would be healed. My natural thoughts, however, leaned toward it happening as a result of an eye transplant, a new powerful medication, surgery, or something else medical. Acie too had always prayed and believed I would see one day. We had both seen him come through so many times in our lives. Like providing for our needs when we were struggling to pay the school bill and when the groceries were delivered to our door or when Acie school bill was paid by someone we didn't know. God truly answered our prayers.

We both knew God could heal. That's what Jesus did when he walked on the earth. He is God and he never changes. If he could do it then, I knew he could do it in our day. We heard reports of God's miracles occurring in our modern times and searched God's Word for deeper understanding.

"For He rescued us from the domain of darkness "(Colossians 1:13). We are to take authority over the devil. "Put on the full armor of God, so that you will be able to stand firm against the schemes of the devil "(Ephesians 6:11). Satan is the one who causes sickness and tragedy.

Yes, I'd been taught to believe God heals in answer to our prayers; however, I hadn't been taught to lay hands on people and expect a miracle where those in bondage are set free. Although biblical, we didn't practice this type of praying. I knew the Word but didn't comprehend its full power. However, my spirit's eyes had been opened for greater understanding and possibilities.

We finally arrived home after midnight on August twenty-sixth. Although exhausted, we never went to bed without Bible reading and prayer. Acie read only two Scripture verses to me before he slipped to his knees for prayer. I was already in bed but closed my eyes out of habit as he prayed.

"Oh God, you can restore Marolyn's eyesight. Lord, I know you can do it. God, I pray you will give Marolyn her eyesight—tonight."

When Acie finished praying I opened my eyes and shouted, "I can see! Acie, I can see!"

"What do you mean?" he asked.

For the first time, I was able to see the face of the man I had married! I could see his rosy checks, and his green eyes. I could see the drapery and details of the room we were in.

"I can see you, Acie! I can see!" I shouted.

"You're kidding," he replied in disbelief, although he'd just concluded his faith-filled prayer, hoping for a miracle. We didn't know anyone who'd received a miracle.

"I'm not kidding, Acie. I can see. I can see the pupils in your eyes. The clock says its one-thirty a.m., and you need a shave. I can see!"

Instantly, the weariness from moments before fell off me like a robe. We jumped up and down, rejoicing and crying at the same time.

"Acie," I said, "I can see the dresser, the bed and the walls ... Oh Acie, I can see the floor, the drapery—everything! I can see! Thank you, Jesus, I can see!"

We both shouted praises and thanks to God.

Acie shook his head in amazement. Grabbing a newspaper, he pointed to the large print at the top of the front page, and asked,

"Can you see this large print?"

"Yes!" I exclaimed. "But I can do better than that. I can read the smaller print! Glory to God, I can read it all!" I remembered how in school I couldn't even see the flame of a cigarette lighter light held six inches from my face. I'd forgotten to spell because I couldn't read words on a page for years. When Acie began his prayer for me, I was completely blind. All I could see was a dark haze. But when I opened my eyes I could see perfectly.

Beside ourselves with happiness and joy, we had a another "hallelujah, Pentecostal" fit.

"This is heaven!" Acie shouted. "It has to be!"

We continued to shout and praise the Lord for what he had done. We shouted until our stomach muscles hurt. Finally, exhausted from the excitement and the late hour, we sat on the bed to relax and take it all in. Such a miracle was overwhelming.

"Honey," Acie asked solemnly, "Do you realize we are on holy ground?"

The awesome thought left us speechless. The realization, the reality of it, hit us both as I looked in the face of the man I married.

"What shall I render to the Lord for all his benefits toward me?" Acie said in humble awe. "Why did I doubt God? I thought I believed, but now I realize I really didn't believe he would do it—an out and out miracle and not through medical science."

For the first time after thirteen years of dating and marrying my husband, I could see him. See his eyes, his nose, his mouth, and his facial expressions. Oh, yes, I liked what I saw. Back in our college days, I remember the girls on campus talked of this good-looking guy named Acie Ford. I could now see for myself, and they were right.

Sharon was at Grandma's that night, but her picture was on the dresser. I grabbed it and stared intently at her features. My baby! She was beautiful with her long, curly, natural-blond hair and blue eyes that showed intelligence and alertness. She showed personality even in her photo. I couldn't wait to see her in person. Oh, to see my husband and my little girl for the first time … no words could describe it.

Did they look as I had pictured them in my mind? My hands had traveled their faces, but neither that nor the descriptions I heard from others could compared to reality. What I pictured for Sharon was close. Her smooth skin, pudgy nose, and bone structure had mostly been "seen" through touch.

But to imagine what a grown man looked like wasn't so easy. His actual appearance did take me by surprise somewhat. But I must say, all in a good way. He had deep green eyes. Even though he was mostly Scotch Irish with light skin, he had a Native American grandmother who had the dark skin and wore braided hair. He had some of her characteristics. His clean-shaven beard grew around the rosy center of his cheeks and gave him a distinguished look. I was pleased with everything about the man God had blessed me with.

Each time I passed the mirror and caught a glimpse of myself, I paused. I could hardly believe how my facial features had changed. I lost my sight at the age of eighteen. Now I was thirty-one. My face had matured and had lost its baby fat.

The joy and elation of that moment was, and still is to this day, almost indescribable. And our hearts overflowed with gratitude to God that he saw us, heard us, and stepped into our situation and revealed his power. Why at that moment and not before? I can't answer that question. What made Acie's passionate prayer that night any different than before? Again, we can't answer this question, but we always trust God's omnipotent power, love, and timing.

Although almost two o'clock a.m., we rushed to call our parents. When the phone rang at my parents' home in Michigan, Mom was awake. She hadn't been able to sleep that night and immediately answered the phone. For years, she had felt helpless and burdened with the thought of my blindness. Our news meant the release of a burden she'd carried all those years. She rejoiced greatly and immediately called my brothers and sisters, waking all of them up in the middle of the night.

Acie phoned his parents and awakened his mother. "Mother, Marolyn can see, Marolyn can see! She can see!" he shouted.

"Acie, is everything all right?" she asked, trying to make sense of his words. She landed into this conversation out of a sound sleep, and undoubtedly had trouble processing what didn't make sense.

Yet, Acie could only repeat over and over the same words, "Mother, Marolyn can see! She can see!"

We made many calls that night. We wanted to tell the world— to run down the street in the middle of the night and shout, "I was blind, but now I can see! It's a miracle! God answered our prayer!"

That day was also Acie's thirty-third birthday. What a gift! We were so excited we talked into the early morning hours, too adrenaline-charged to sleep. Although he had to work the next day, he said later he was afraid to go to sleep … afraid he might wake up to find this had all been a dream. Exhaustion finally overtook us, however, and we slept an hour or two.

The next morning, the first words out of Acie's mouth were, "Marolyn, is it true? Can you see? Or was I dreaming?"

"It was no dream, Acie. I can see everything."

GOD SAID YES!

As I looked out the window, words couldn't express the beauty. I hadn't seen the outdoors clearly in years. The miracle of the morning sun later gave way to raindrops and puddles, pooling and soaking into dry ground. I marveled at all of it. The individual blades of grass, the leaves blowing in the wind was all so wonderful. My heart rose with praise to see God's creation on that first day.

Acie called his boss first thing and shared the news. By now, he was calmer than when he talked to his mother the night before. "Mr. Moses, Marolyn can see. My wife's eyesight has come back, and it happened on my birthday." He was hoping he could have the day off to rejoice with me.

"That's wonderful, Acie, but get to work as soon as you can."

Acie did as Mr. Moses suggested and was only five minutes late for work. When he arrived at the store, everyone had been talking, wondering about the miracle. From the minute he walked in, all the employees' eyes were on him. They wanted to hear more about it. They were excited and happy with him. He had an impossible task of keeping his mind on selling clothing. While waiting on customers, he told them about our miracle. He couldn't help himself and he couldn't wipe the smile off his face.

"My wife was blind," he shared repeatedly. "God did a miracle last night. He touched Marolyn's eyes, and she can see."

While it could've upset his boss, the customers wanted to hear more of the story, so they stayed in the store longer and ended up buying more. It turned out to be a good day for the business.

News of the miracle spread quickly throughout the community. Throughout the day, the house filled with friends and neighbors asking, "Is it true? Is it true?"

"Yes, yes, yes." Happily, I recounted over and over again how the miracle happened through prayer—a simple one-minute prayer. Like a revolving door, a steady stream of people came and went, and a continual celebration where God received all the glory filled our home.

Although I wished Acie could be at home that day, maybe God wanted him to share with his coworkers and the many shoppers of this powerful witness of God's mighty acts. While Acie rejoiced with the shoppers, he kept looking at his watch. He truly wanted to be home.

At two o'clock in the afternoon, he called me with great excitement in his voice. "Marolyn, can you still see?"

He called home not only that day but for several more days with the same question. "Can you still see?"

He didn't doubt the miracle. It was so amazing and wonderful, he could hardly take in. Part of us felt a little fearful that my new sight would only be temporary. In fact, some of the more skeptical people warned us that my sight might be just temporary. We didn't accept those negative words but continued to praise God for his wonderful gift of sight.

When we called Mom and Dad Ford during the night to tell them what God had done, they didn't wake up Sharon. They planned to tell her during breakfast, but when she sat down at the table, cranky from a late night, they decided to wait until they were in the car driving her back to our house.

GOD SAID YES!

"Oh goodie, I can put up my mop and broom," Sharon said in the car that day. "I won't have to help mommy with the floors anymore."

When I found out what she said, I realized the undo pressure I'd put on Sharon as a child, although God used it to develop compassion and maturity in her character.

Mom and Dad Ford arrived late in the afternoon with our daughter who was now nearly five. By that time, our driveway and church parking lot were full, with cars spilling out to the roadside. One of the ladies in our packed house came up to me smiling.

"Acie's parents have parked on the roadside and are coming up the driveway with Sharon."

Bursting out the door, I ran up the driveway with outstretched arms. I hollered, "Sharon, Sharon, I can see you! I can see what you look like."

I was finally able to take in her long, curly blonde hair, her deep blue eyes, and her light complexion. She was beautiful. Tears streamed down her face.

"Mommy can you really see?"

My precious little girl had carried the weight of my blindness her entire life. Finally, she would know what it was like to have a mommy who could see.

23

Although my ophthalmologist's schedule was full, when he heard about my miracle, he asked me to come in so he could see what happened. As I sat in his big black chair staring at the big "E" at the top of the eye chart, I smiled. I could read everything from the top of the chart all the way to the smallest print at the bottom.

The doctor peered into my eyes with his light scope for what seemed like forever, never uttering a word. I held my breath, waiting.

A man of few words, he finally spoke. "Marolyn, your eyes are still the same. Nothing has changed medically. According to what I see, you should still be blind. It's medically impossible for you to see."

"We serve a mighty God," I said.

Sometime later, I attended a funeral, and the eye doctor's assistant happened to be there. She pulled me aside and told me the following story.

"Marolyn, you don't know me," she said, "but I've got to tell you what happened the day you came in to see the doctor after your miracle. My job was to follow the doctor back into his office after he saw a patient, and he would dictate to me what to write down on the patient's medical record. I would take it in shorthand and later type it out. Well, that day after the doctor said he didn't know how you were seeing, we went to his office, and he leaned back in his chair in total silence. He sat there for like twenty minutes, and I felt really uncomfortable. I didn't know if I should leave the room or keep waiting for his dictation.

"Finally, he looked up and said, 'I don't know how that lady is seeing. I don't know what to tell you for her record. I've never seen anything like this.'"

Our lives changed in so many ways from that moment on. Major newspapers picked up the story, and it circulated nationwide. Indeed, a true miracle of biblical proportions had taken place.

For days Acie asked, "Marolyn, can you see as good as you could the day after the miracle?"

"Yes, yes, Acie, I can see as well as when God gave me sight. It's for keeps."

Over the years, much of the scar tissue in the back of my eyes gradually disappeared, but some damaged scar tissue remained in both eyes. In other words, this wasn't merely a healing but a miracle.

People wanted to hear more about this miracle, and doors of opportunity opened for me to share my story. Perhaps this was the start of what I'd envisioned all those years ago on the farm under the clothesline.

After I began speaking in the great crusade meetings, the Lord brought to my memory that vision he gave me at a young age while worshipping him out on the lawn. I stood in awe of God's marvelous working in my life. Those thirteen years of blindness were now being used for God's eternal purpose. Jesus set me free and is still using it for His glory today.

24

From Test to Testimony

Two weeks after the miracle, I was asked to speak at a Baptist Bicentennial Church Celebration, the Rev. Paul Carter, pastor. Over five-hundred people attended, including around sixty ministers and their wives. I accepted the invitation but was petrified at the thought of speaking in front of that many people. Yet, in my heart I knew this really wasn't about me but about Jesus. He was real and alive. I was merely a clay vessel, cracked and marred, simply available for him to pour through. He would do it. Besides, how could I *not* tell others of the wonder he'd done? I had to speak regardless of my fears. I wanted to tell the world. I had to.

As nervous as I was to stand in front of all those people, God didn't leave me alone. I felt his presence, and when the first few words stumbled out of my mouth, he loosened my tongue and delivered me from the fear of speaking publicly. Soon, the story rolled out effortlessly. God's Spirit poured out on the congregation that day. Several pastors in attendance invited me to share my testimony with their congregations in the days and weeks that followed.

The floodgates were opened, and requests came pouring in. It seemed almost daily I was being asked to go somewhere to tell what God had done for me. No publicity, no advertising. All I had to do was answer my phone.

After healing the demoniac of Gadara, Jesus said to him, "Go home to your people and report to them what great things the Lord has done for you, and how He had mercy on you" (Mark 5:19). That's all I was doing.

And God used this miracle to cross denominational lines. Everybody from Baptists, Catholics, Methodists, Presbyterians, Pentecostals, to Charismatics—all desperately needed to be encouraged that God was really alive and still doing miracles today. Little did I realize this would be the birth of the *Marolyn Ford Ministries*, an international ministry to bring glory to God's amazing power. Over the next two and half decades, God took me around the world, speaking to churches and crusade meetings of up to thirty thousand people in attendance.

I appeared on television shows like the *700 Club*, the *PTL Club*, and *the James Robinson Show*, and did many other TV interviews in other countries. Some of these shows had me on multiple times. God wanted me to tell my story, and he made it happen.

What had been the most difficult thing in my life was now my platform for ministry. God had turned my tribulation, which was the testing of my faith and endurance, into a message of healing that glorified God, the Maker of heaven and earth, by whom all things exist.

Because the miracle was so real and profound with medical documentation, Acie and I wanted to visit the Training Center for the Blind in Arkansas to let them hear firsthand what God had done. We had a wonderful time visiting with our friends there. Many of the workers were amazed, but those in authority asked that we not share the healing miracle with the trainees out of concern for those who might question, "Why them and not me?" They might be tempted to go home and wait on their miracle rather than learning Braille.

As we were talking in the front foyer, a nice-looking, young blind man with a briefcase walked right into a wall. My heart broke for him. Except for the grace of God, that could've been me. Why had I been healed while others I knew who'd been praying and trusting God for their miracle were still waiting? I couldn't answer that question.

Sometimes God doesn't heal or deliver us, and we don't know why. It's in those times we must do as Proverbs 3:5 says. "Trust in the Lord with all your heart and do not lean on your own understanding." It's not because of any lack of faith on our part and doesn't mean God is disappointed in us or doesn't love us or feel our pain. He has his eternal reasons to perform a sovereign act as a gift for his eternal purposes.

John the Baptist, whom Jesus said was the greatest man who had ever lived (Matthew 11:11) was not delivered out of prison and was beheaded, though he sought deliverance greatly. Every one of the disciples were not delivered and died atrocious deaths—not because of their lack of faith.

One thing I knew for sure, I had a responsibility to be faithful with the gift God had given me. He's willing and able to heal, though it was difficult to keep trusting in him and standing on his promises when years pass and seemingly nothing happened. I could never give up. Jesus told his disciples "that at all times they ought to pray and not to lose heart" (Luke 18:1). God's will is sovereign.

I believe God has given each of us unique abilities and talents to use for His glory. Each of us has a destiny to fulfill. I had to ask myself, "What are the dreams and desires of my heart? What am I able to do with the abilities I possess? Whether healed or not, God would give me an open door to fulfill his purpose for my being on earth. By His sovereign grace I was healed. Those years of being blind were not in vain. They were a part of God's plan to send me around the world sharing my story.

A couple months after my blind eyes were opened, we experienced another answer to prayer. Acie and I had prayed for more than a year for God to move us from the bivocational church to a full-time pastoral position. About that time, a friend, Rev. Michael Howard, a wonderful pastor in Felsenthal, Arkansas, felt impressed to give Acie's name to the chairman of the pulpit committee of the First Baptist Church of Huttig, Arkansas. This would be a full-time pastoral position.

As Reverend Howard shared with us some of the particulars about the church and the position, Acie and I prayed about whether this was God's place for us. The more we prayed, the more we felt the Lord was opening this door. So, by the time the pulpit committee came to hear him preach, we already knew the next place for him to pastor would be at that church. The committee also felt God's leading and offered Acie the position.

After serving the Crossroads church for four years, we packed and said our tearful goodbyes to our wonderful congregation, closing a special chapter in our lives. They had walked with us through many of those challenging years while I was blind and struggling to rear Sharon. They'd seen the miracle of my sight being restored that changed our lives drastically. We had blessed memories there with them. As we hugged and talked, I could see their faces and recorded them in my mind.

Mixed with the tears of making our departure were tears of joy and great excitement. Acie was moving into full-time ministry.

I looked forward to our first move where I could actually see our new house and decorate it the way I wished. I would never take these small things for granted again—ever.

Our new congregation in Huttig, Arkansas, had built a beautiful home for the pastor's family that matched the church building. We were blessed to be the first family to live in it. Huge trees hovered over the street. Everything in the church and city was neat and well kept.

Acie preached his heart out on Sundays and was able to be on the church field serving God and the people every day, all day. He loved the ministry responsibilities, the visitation, and even the children's Daily Vacation Bible School and telling them Bible stories. The church had no other staff. I worked again with the music and directed the choir. I'd been responsible for those at the Crossroads church, so I pick up where I left off. In addition, I also became the church secretary. We loved the people and our ministry there. Acie was serving in a church as full-time pastor, which satisfied the longing of his heart.

After a year, we were finally able to drive up to Holland, Michigan, to see my family. I hadn't seen the face of my parents, brothers, and sisters in thirteen years.

While we were in Holland, God opened the door for me to share my testimony of God's miracle in my home church, the Immanuel Baptist Church. The sanctuary was filled to capacity, and folks had to find seating in an area below the sanctuary. Many of these friends and relatives who came that night had been praying for me for years. The visit filled my soul in so many ways. To be with family and friends like that was such a blessing. Getting to actually see them was the icing on the cake. I loved them dearly and recognized this was their miracle too because of their prayers for me.

The delight of that unforgettable visit can't be expressed in mere words. I will always be grateful for that window of time. A year later, my father passed away unexpectedly. How grateful I was to have been blessed to see his face that one time before his passing.

Over the six years of ministry in Huttig, my life became fast paced as I tried to juggle my role as pastor's wife, mother, music director, and traveling speaker. The invitations to share God's miracle kept pouring in. Soon, flying became my weekly routine since sharing God's wonderful gift of restored vision was God's call upon my life. It became necessary for us to move on to serve a church that had a full staff and secretaries to handle the work. I needed to be relieved of my responsibilities in order to travel more freely as God opened the doors of opportunity for me.

Acie had been asked by a pulpit committee to send in his résumé to the Boulevard Church in Memphis, Tennessee. We couldn't figure how they heard of him, but after sending his résumé, we didn't hear back from them for a year. We learned later that they had misplaced his résumé. We remained faithful to the work in Huttig until we could relocate.

25

We Nearly Lost You in Surgery

We experienced four more miscarried pregnancies after Sharon was born. One was six months along.

Seven years after her birth, I endured tremendous pain for six weeks, thinking my monthly was going to be hard, as usual. The pain grew in intensity until I couldn't stand the pain any longer and had to find out if something might be wrong. I called for an emergency appointment. The doctor was able to work me in.

Upon examining me, he simply said, "You're pregnant, and the egg has adhered to the inside of one of your fallopian tube. It has begun to rupture. You need surgery."

A tubal pregnancy can never grow to term. Once the egg grows past the size of the tube in which it was contained, it ruptures, ending the pregnancy and creating an emergency medical situation for the mother. The tube ruptured, spreading poison throughout my body. Now, in the emergency room, the doctors fought for my life.

For a good while after the surgery, my whole body trembled. At my six-week checkup, I asked the doctor, "Why am I shaking like this?"

"We nearly lost you in surgery," he responded. "Your body went into shock. You'll be shaky for a good while, but you'll overcome it with time."

Both Acie and I were relieved and thankful I'd survived, yet we grieved the loss of another child. We were devastated. Again, the doctor commented that miscarriages were God's way of taking care of something that was bad. I still couldn't believe this was supposed to console us.

Years earlier, I was told I had developed endometriosis. This is what led to my need for a hysterectomy which meant I could never bear any more children. I'd always desired to have a large family, but God had a different plan for my life.

I take comfort in knowing that had I kept all those children I wouldn't have been free to travel as extensively as I did over the years of sharing God's miracle. Jesus told one man who was healed to go show himself to the priest. And that's what he had me do—make my ministry known to all denominations around the world.

The invitations for me to share my story kept coming from the ministers who heard me speak in the crusade meetings of God's miraculous healing power. I flew constantly from one city to the next. Neither of us were accustomed to this new lifestyle. Acie would pick me up at the airport with a welcome-home hug and shower me with kisses. My absence was difficult on both of us at first, but he was thrilled with my opportunities to share God's miracle. Because he loved his own ministry work, he never complained about my schedule—at least not to me.

Perhaps nothing demonstrated his support better than the time we were driving home from the Monroe, Louisiana, airport, and he told me of his work on the church field and events that had transpired while I was away. In turn, I told him about my meetings and how God had blessed and changed lives. What he said next took me by surprise.

"I'll never complain about your being gone, not ever again!"

"Acie, you've never complained about my travels," I replied in surprise.

"I haven't complained to you," he responded honestly, "but I sure let the Lord know I didn't like you being gone so much."

"Do you not want me to continue my ministry and traveling?" I asked.

"Yes, oh, yes, I do," he replied without hesitation. "While you were gone, I had a dream in which the Lord asked me, 'Would you rather have a wife who is blind or one who can see and tell this wonderful story as my witness?' It opened my eyes." Acie took a long breath and hugged me tightly. "I'll never complain again about your being gone. You go anywhere God opens a door."

We both knew God had put a call upon my life, and the pastoral ministry was Acie's calling. Fulfilling our callings and reaching our destinies wasn't always comfortable. Many of my evangelist friends said they hated the traveling part; they'd rather be at home with their wife and family and in their own beds, but they felt compelled to fulfill God's call upon their life, which was to preach the Word. Acie and I also didn't like the separation part and would rather have been together.

"I believe God established my thoughts through that dream," Acie explained.

My ministry was never an issue for him again. God had opened doors for me to share what he did in my life, and Acie supported that one hundred percent. I could barely put into words what a blessing it was to have a godly, adapting, loving husband. That's why I never stayed away from home to sightsee while away on speaking engagements, and I tried to balance my speaking ministry with my family life. I always caught the earliest flight back home so I'd have the day with my Acie and Sharon and be about my church work.

Once, a ministerial friend asked Acie, "How do you cope with your wife being asked to speak at all these big conference meetings and being with the great men of God while you remained at the home front? Some men would feel challenged or jealous if their wife had a worldwide ministry while they stayed home."

"That never bothers me," he explained. "I love having my wife in ministry. I feel it's an extension of my ministry."

Wow! What a beautiful attitude. He was always so proud of me.

Working as a team and supporting each other's gifts and callings had been the core of our relationship. I praise God for a husband like Acie. His support enabled me to embrace God's call on my life with every fiber of my being. He was truly in this with me one hundred percent.

Whenever we faced a challenge, Acie and I went to prayer. Mentally and emotionally, we agreed I'd travel wherever God opened the door, yet because of where we lived my treks around the country challenged us in more ways than one. It was a two-hour round trip from our home to get to the airport in Monroe, which wasn't a major hub. I then had to catch a flight to one of the larger airports—either Memphis, Dallas, or Atlanta—and from there, catch another flight to wherever I had a meeting. Each trip involved at least two, sometimes three, flights to get to my destination which physically drained me and consumed a lot of time.

After six years of traveling back and forth to this small airport, Acie and I were still praying for God to move us closer to one of the major airports so we could reduce my travel time. We learned later that the Boulevard pulpit committee had misplaced Acie's résumé. After having worked through all the résumés they received, one of the men spoke up and said, 'Wasn't there a résumé from a pastor down in Louisiana? What happened to him and where is his résumé?" The search was on.

In answer to our prayers, God used Bill Strickland, a man whom we weren't yet acquainted with but who'd once heard my testimony when I spoke at the La Belle Haven Baptist Church in Memphis. He was the man who had given Acie's résumé to that pulpit committee. This church was located practically at the door of the Memphis International Airport. What a blessed answer to our prayers! Once again, God showed us he was in control of our lives.

Memphis would be our home for the next thirty-five years, and Acie expanded his influence and became the pastor of the Boulevard Baptist Church with seven staff members working under him. I no longer needed to work with the church ministries like I'd done in our prior churches, thus freeing me up for a much greater ministry. God called Acie to pastor this church because they had a difficult preexisting problem. God needed him there to guide and direct them through that difficult transition. In the years to come, God used him in a mighty way throughout the city of Memphis. Having guided the church through the problem, Acie was ready for another pastoral move.

Broadmoor Church, an hour's drive on the north side of the city, later extended a call to Acie to become associate pastor working under Dr. Jack May, who later was voted president of the Tennessee Baptist Convention. Aice was voted vice president and later president of the Shelby Baptist Association and worked on several committees over the thirty-five years we lived in

Memphis. Acie and Dr. May were well acquainted with one another.

God also continued to expand *Marolyn Ford Ministries* beyond measure. The overseas ministries had begun. Having been asked to share my testimony at the Southern Baptist Convention held in Atlanta, the ministry grew beyond what I could imagine.

Twenty-five years had passed since the day of the miracle of restored sight, and I could still see perfectly. My baby girl, Sharon, had grown into a beautiful young woman. God had allowed me to minister through sharing God's healing miracle and teaching on faith and the power of God to answer prayer in conferences, universities, churches, club meetings, radio, and TV interviews at home and abroad.

Truly, God was fulfilling the vision as it was revealed to me when I was a young girl under the clothesline.

PART II
Miracle II

26

SHE'S BROKEN AND ...

I had stolen away for one of those rare moments of relaxation to soak in our Jacuzzi hot tub at home. When I stepped out of the tub onto the rough marble step, my foot slipped out from under me as if on glass. My lower back hit the long waterspout as I fell back into the water. A loud thud reverberated up the hallway.

"Marolyn! Honey!" Acie shouted as he came running down the hallway and into the bedroom. "What happened?"

"I'm okay, but my back is going to be badly bruised from top to bottom," I said with tears in my eyes, my body throbbing. "Thank God I didn't hit my head on the marble shelf." I made a feeble attempt to explain what happened while trembling and struggling unsuccessfully to get to my feet.

Acie helped me up and draped a towel around me, my feet still in the water, and snuggled me into his loving arms.

He told me later that in that solemn moment as he was holding me tightly, he heard the Holy Spirit whisper in his ear, "She's broken, and you're going to have to take care of her." Acie had no idea what it meant.

After all, I told him I'd be all right.

With his strong arms and loving care, he helped me get dried off and my pj's on. As he tucked me into bed, our plans for the evening were curtailed.

The next morning, I could barely move, and my backside was black and blue. Acie took me to the doctor, and we described the accident and injury.

"It is obvious Marolyn is in severe pain," he said without ordering an X-ray. "I suggest she take some over-the-counter medicine for relief. If she isn't better tomorrow, bring her back in. I'll be leaving to go overseas, but my associate will be happy to see her."

I sensed I needed an X-ray, MRI, or possibly surgery right then but didn't want to suggest it. So, I remained silent.

Acie located a wheelchair at the front door and wheeled me out of the office to the car. With every move, the pain became more excruciating. I couldn't walk. At the time, I wasn't overly concerned. I'd hit my back hard, and the swelling was to be expected. We assumed that after a few days everything would be back to normal.

Two weeks passed, but things didn't get better.

On Sunday morning, Acie asked a different doctor, who was also a member of our church and friend of the family, if he would come by the house and evaluate my situation after the church service.

He asked me to perform simple leg movements.

I failed miserably, thinking the swelling was impeding my ability to move.

The doctor looked at Acie and shook his head. "Time isn't going to heal this," he explained. "Marolyn needs to get to the hospital immediately."

He called for an ambulance and arranged for a bone specialist to meet us at the emergency room. For the next four hours, I lay in the examining room on a cold, steel table with no pad or cushion to soften the pain.

In agony, tears filled my eyes as I said to Acie, "I can't lie here on this hard table any longer. Maybe the doctor forgot about me."

About thirty-five to-forty minutes before the doctor arrived, the pain disappeared, replaced by a new sensation—numbness. Rather than being concerned, I was more thankful for the absence of pain and considered it a blessed relief.

Another hour passed when a bone specialist finally came in to examine me. He moved my legs up and down to check my mobility. A few minutes earlier, I would have screamed in pain from the movement but now was completely numb. I felt nothing—no pain, no discomfort. Except, I was so cold to the point my teeth were chattering. Barely able to talk, I let Acie fill the doctor in on the details of the accident.

The doctor ordered a CT scan which revealed I had crushed the fifth lumbar vertebrae in my lower back. They wheeled me into a hospital room and scheduled me for surgery four days later. Once settled in my room with blankets to warm me, the pain burst back on the scene.

The next morning, the doctor came into my room, pulled up a chair next to the bed and looked me straight in the eyes. I'll never forget his stern words.

"Following the surgery, you will get out of this bed and sit in that chair. You will walk up and down these hallways. And there will be no getting out of it. No self-pity party. You understand?"

All I could do was nod in compliance.

Maybe the doctor spoke to me that way because I had Acie talk to him for me when in the emergency room. I wasn't taking the initiative to speak for myself because my teeth were still trembling—I was so cold. After he left, his words continued to reverberate in my mind. It felt like he was scolding me or prejudging my future behavior. When the nurse came in later to check my vitals, I expressed my dismay over his remarks.

"Is he that way with all his patients?" I asked.

"I don't know what his problem is," she replied. "He's normally not like that."

Then his behavior turned even more confusing. At eleven-thirty the evening before my surgery, a nurse came into the room and asked me to sign some papers for a different doctor to do the surgery.

"Why does he want to be removed from my case?" I asked as I signed the papers and handed them back to her.

"He felt he got off to a wrong start with you and wanted to back away," she explained.

I figured the nurse must've told him I'd asked about his communication with me two days prior. However, to my surprise, after the surgery he came to check on me and apologized for his odd behavior.

"I was there to observe the doctor as he did your surgery. The damage to your back was far worse than we could see on the CT scan," he said. "You must have taken quite a fall. There were fragments of crushed bone everywhere. The surgeon had to remove the splinters one piece at a time. Some were difficult to remove, but we feel all have been safely removed, and you should have complete recovery."

Maybe that's why he backed off from doing the surgery. I never knew. I accepted his apology and said nothing more about it. But I took comfort in understanding a little more of what had happened to the crushed firth lumbar vertebrae. I appreciated his kindness to fill me in on what they had to do during the surgery to remove the splinters.

Later, I learned that the fifth vertebrae is where the nerves connect to the colon and bladder. It didn't seem that important then, but it had affected everything.

It quickly became apparent that my colon wasn't working, even while I was still in the hospital. The surgeon showed absolutely no concern for my colon problem. Four days later, I was dismissed from the hospital.

After my release, I made an appointment with a gastroenterologist who, after examining me, suggested I begin taking enemas and gave me the name of another gastroenterologist I should see.

He, too, didn't know how to treat me and sent to me yet another gastroenterologist. I was on now the verge of despair.

Days passed, and I scheduled yet another appointment with a third gastro specialist. This couldn't go on any longer. I needed help. I arrived hopeful this doctor would have an answer for my colon and bladder problems.

After performing numerous tests and X-rays in his office that day, he sat down with Acie and me and gave us yet more devastating news. "Your problem is complicated and more than I can handle. Your condition is quite serious. I'm referring you to an autonomic nervous system specialist, Dr. Thomas Abell at the University of Tennessee Medical Research Center, Bowld Hospital. It's a research center."

That sounded hopeful to me. I needed immediate help from someone.

"Let me see if I can get an appointment for you to see him this afternoon," he said.

I nodded. He sounded certain this was the doctor I needed to see. I was thankful someone knew who to send me to and was willing to try to get an appointment for me quickly.

They had an opening, and I felt blessed to have this appointment with a doctor located in Memphis who was doing research on rats in the area with which I was having difficulty. Maybe he'd be able to find the cause and get things working again. I was suffering in agonizing pain and nervous about being passed around like a hot potato from one doctor to another and getting no help and no relief.

After my first meeting with Dr. Thomas Abell, I knew he'd be able to help me. His research specialized in autonomic disorder of the digestive track. Immediately, he scheduled me to undergo extensive medical procedures and tests several times weekly over the following months. I wanted a quick fix, but he made no mention of hope or possible surgery.

When the tests began, I had no idea what I was in for. The testing continued, unending month after month. These procedures were terribly painful, invasive, and physically draining.

27

Paralysis and Paralyzing Fear

Nothing was worse than hearing my doctor say, "I don't know how to help you."

The fall had affected my digestive system, which wasn't working. This drastically changed my daily routine. The complex natural functions of my body, which I'd always taken for granted, were now up to me to perform manually with enemas, self-catheters, and other time-consuming and difficult routines.

For the first time I considered the unthinkable. *What if I didn't don't get better? What if I have to live like this the rest of my life?* Extreme chronic pain and misery now became my constant companion.

My schedule was booked full of speaking engagements for the next twenty-four months. I was determined to keep going. Though I could barely still walk, I had to. Something inside my core sensed if I stopped pushing forward, stopped telling my story of what God had done, I *would* die. I struggled to maintain a positive outlook as my life spiraled out of my control.

Had God miraculously healed my blind eyes and fulfilled the vision he gave me when I was sitting on the lawn that day when I was young, only to let it be taken away like this?

The enemy was trying to stop me.

So, despite the ordeal and pain, I had to work these medical procedures around my speaking schedule somehow. I did my best to fulfill as many of my obligations as possible, but many had to be canceled or rescheduled.

As my physical energy drained, so did my emotional energy. As with my blindness, my quality of life and freedom had again been stolen from me overnight.

The constant stress of being my caregiver started to take a toll on Acie too. We both were physically, emotionally, and spiritually exhausted. Weeks of tests with no positive results had plunged my typically positive attitude into the basement at times. Each negative report sent me reeling further into despair. The fear that gripped my soul was like a vice squeezing me. I felt completely paralyzed. When I was blind, at least I could help myself. Now I was helpless, and my body was getting weaker each day.

Finally, after months of medical testing, Dr. Abell was able to diagnose my condition. I had what was called a *totally paralyzed digestive system*. After running more test and procedures, he learned that my entire digestive system wasn't working—at all. This meant the involuntary nerves and muscle contractions of my urinary and GI tract had stopped functioning entirely.

"Most people who suffer with some type of digestive failure at least have parts of the colon still working," Dr. Abell said. "In your case, nothing is working. I don't even have a medical term for it to know how to enter it in your medical records. I'll have to come up with a name for it."

For lack of anything better, he officially diagnosed me with Total Paralyzed Digestive System Autonomic Disorder. This also affected the pelvic floor muscles, bladder, and later the stomach and esophagus muscles.

God had told Acie, "She's broken, and you'll have to take care of her."

Our lives would never be the same again.

GOD SAID YES!

The ensuing battle in my mind drifted between faith and doubt as I questioned the truth of God's Word on this issue of his healing power. Would God be willing to heal me a second time? Could I really believe? "Who heals all your diseases" (Psalm 103:3)?

After I experienced the miracle of restoration of my eyesight, I would've thought my faith would've been as solid as a rock. But the battle now before me loomed bigger and more overwhelming than my blindness had been. The continued medical reports revealed this was a matter of life and death. I wondered within myself whether God would accept my prayers because I questioned his willingness to heal me a second time.

Did that mean I was questioning his omnipotent power? These thoughts erected a barrier to my faith. They robbed me of my energy, my hope of life itself. and drove me into despair. I struggled greatly over this for several weeks. My fear overrode my knowledge of Scripture and my confidence in God.

I was afraid for life itself, but also afraid because I felt this way—doubting and questioning God. I had to work through these doubts and fears, and it wasn't easy. I had to take control of my thoughts before they destroyed me. But how? I knew the truth. I had experienced a bonafide miracle with my eyesight restored. What God promised; he would do.

The cross gave me access to all his exceeding great and precious promises. The underlining question was, would he? Could I believe and expect God to do something so great and wonderful for me a second time? I wrestled with that for several weeks.

By an act of my will, I had to make the decision to stand on God's Word. "For as the rain and the snow come down from heaven, And do not return there without watering the earth And making it bear and sprout, And furnishing seed to the sower and

145

bread to the eater; So will My word be which goes forth from My mouth: It will not return to Me empty, without accomplishing what I desire, And without succeeding *in the matter* for which I sent it" (Isaiah 55:10-11). That became God's promise to me personally. Believing the Word calmed my spirit and brought peace to my soul. Tough times were upon me, but God had warned us that tough times would come. I buckled back into a place of faith and trust in the God who created the heavens and the earth.

One of the biggest changes I made regarded the words I spoke. Maybe not so much as to what I said but to what I didn't say. I once heard a quote that said, "Just as faith produces things desired, fear produces things not desired."

I had to take control of my thought life. After hearing some of the medical reports from my doctor, I could've easily said, "Most likely I'm going to die with this illness," but I never did. Instead, I had to change my thoughts which changed my words.

"For as he thinks within himself, so he is" (Prov. 23:7). I had to let faith fill my heart and the Word fill my mind and guard against words of fear and doubt. The words we speak are very important because they become seeds planted in our spirit, and they create a harvest after their kind.

I had to make a deliberate decision that I would stand on and trust God's Word for my healing.

28

A POLICEMAN SENT FROM GOD!

My urology specialist explained I would need urinal self-catheters, which would allow me to eliminate the fluids from my bladder, and he handed me a prescription for them. Upon leaving his office, desperately in need of relief, I rushed to the nearest drugstore to fill the prescription. The druggist informed me that my prescription could only be filled by a medical supply house, and they were closed for the weekend. This was bad news.

I took a deep breath to calm my anxiety. My only choice was to make a mad dash to the hospital emergency room for their assistance.

My body was a ticking time bomb. In agonizing pain, I exited the drug store and headed for my car, expecting to head for the hospital like a woman in labor. I almost reached the car, when a young woman stepped in front of me. She didn't look happy.

"You hit my car when you pulled into that parking space," she said with an attitude. "I've already called the police who are on their way here. You better not leave, or I will charge you with a hit and run."

Oh no! This can't be happening! God, please help! Sitting in my car waiting, I thought I would pass out from the pressure on my bladder. When the bladder can't eliminate, it poisons our insides. Finally, a policeman arrived thirty minutes later. After he talked with the young girl for what seemed like hours, he walked over to me.

"May I see your driver's license?" he asked, holding out his hand. As I handed him my license, he looked at it briefly and commented. "Are you aware that this young girl here is your neighbor? She lives across the street from you."

"No, I wasn't aware of that," I replied, wanting to be on my way. When he mentioned her last name, I realized I was familiar with her parents, but I didn't know their daughter.

"Officer," I said, "I'm in severe pain."

I gave him a brief run-down of my need to get the catheters and asked if he could come by the hospital emergency room later to clear this up.

He walked around my car to look at the paint job, came back and said, "It's quite obvious that your car didn't hit her car as she claims. She is falsely accusing you. I'll have to ask you to stay just a little longer before you can leave the scene."

By this time, the pain was so severe, saliva was running down my teeth. After he talked further and finished up with the young lady, she pulled out, and he came back to my car,

"My wife has serious bladder problems and has to use the self-catheters. I gave her a call, and she would like to give you enough catheters and medical supplies to get you through the weekend. She can tell you things you may not know about using the catheters and urinal leg bags."

With that, he handed me his wife's name, address, and phone number.

"She's expecting your call. You can go."

What a God thing! What first appeared to be misfortune turned out to be God's provision. The policeman was a raven sent by God. As it turned out, he saved me a hospital emergency room bill which was also a blessing from God.

The difficulty I had learning how to use the catheters was horrendous. At this point, I was still mobile, though unsure as to how I would adjust to all this new medical equipment. Pushing myself to maintain some of my speaking schedule, both stateside and internationally, was good for me.

My overseas trip was upon me. I didn't need to cancel it; I simply needed to learn how to deal with and use the new medical equipment, which was difficult for me. I thought I could do that, regardless of whether at home or away. I quickly discovered airplanes and airport facilities weren't conducive for performing the self-catheterization now required in my daily routine. I hadn't been told about the necessity of a urinal leg bag while traveling. I thought the self-catheter would suffice, but I quickly learned a lot about my travel needs on that trip to London.

While overseas, I purchase large supplies of water not only for drinking but for these daily enema functions as well.

In the midst of all this, I was already at a high stress level and couldn't handle any more nerve-wracking events. Physically and mentally, I wondered how I would ever keep going like this.

Like my mother always said, "When there is a will, there is a way."

Fighting back the tears in the airport, I prayed, *God, help me ... please.*

Had I some privacy, I would've burst into tears and hard screams. But I pulled myself together, and with God's help, by the time I reached my destination in London and got a good night's rest, I was ready to share with the people my miracle story of how God had healed my blind eyes, and I taught God's Word.

As I returned home, I remained under great stress trying to cope with the horrible illness still new to me, not knowing whether I would live or die with it.

29

Unexpected Tragedy

By now, Sharon had been happily married to her wonderful husband, John, for a little over a year. They were a perfect match for each other and were very much in love.

He was a military man, and they had purchased a house in Dover, Kentucky, a forty-five-minute drive from Fort Campbell where he was stationed.

Sharon was in the early part of the second trimester of pregnancy with their first child. Four months after they moved, John's platoon received orders to go to Germany. He had a tough time leaving, but Sharon had a harder time letting him go.

Separation for military families is difficult even when not in war time. Sharon had challenges in the pregnancy which made their separation especially hard for her. We arranged for her to stay with us during the days prior to delivery. The baby would be born at the Millington Naval Base Hospital. John had been given a leave to come home for the delivery.

She'd been given a different doctor for each month's pregnancy checkup at the military hospital with no continuity in her prenatal care and little attention given to the challenges she encountered during her pregnancy.

I went with her to see the doctor on her last doctor's visit before the baby would be born. She'd been concerned over her weight gain for months, but she couldn't get the doctors she'd seen to take her seriously. Each of these different doctors, not having seen her before, evidently took for granted that she had a weight problem prior to her pregnancy, but she didn't. This weight problem wasn't normal for her. She couldn't get them to understand that.

On this particular visit, Sharon demanded they check her blood.

"I've been telling you every month that I am toxic, and I'm not going home this time until you check my blood," Sharon stated.

Finally, they listened to her and tested her blood. She was extremely toxic.

"We need to do a C-Section. Prep her for surgery—now!" the doctor shouted.

Immediately, I telephoned John and Acie to tell them Sharon was going into emergency surgery. We anxiously bided our time in the surgical waiting room for the doctor to come out of the delivery room.

He sent word to us. "We could lose both lives in delivery. We might be able to save one life, but it's unlikely we'll be able to save them both. We'll do the best we can."

We immediately went into prayer and cried out to God to spare both their lives. The minutes ticked by slowly in a never-ending sort of time warp as we awaited further news in tense anticipation.

Finally, a military doctor came walking toward us. "Both have survived the delivery. Both baby and mother are stable and doing well," he said.

"Oh, thank God! Thank you, thank you!" We praised God for his mercy in sparing both Sharon and the baby.

"Can we see them?" we asked.

GOD SAID YES!

"Yes, when we get through. We'll let you know when you can go in," he said.

Our first grandchild, Sawyer Roberts, made his entrance into the world. God had answered our prayers. The moment was overwhelming, realizing both lives had been spared, and both were still with us. We thanked God again and rejoiced over his protection.

Acie saw the baby before I did, and he was beaming from ear to ear.

Holding the baby, I thanked God I had my sight and could see my grandbaby. I could hardly contain my excitement. I kissed his little hands and feet as I counted his fingers and toes and snuggled up to his soft cheeks and red hair. He was built just like his daddy—tall and slender. Watching our daughter enter into this new season of life as a mother, our hearts burst with joy.

The time flew by quickly, and within two weeks John had to return to his unit in Germany to finish his duties there.

Six months later, when his stint overseas was completed, he was able to return home from Germany. They were together again.

He was tationed now at the base in Ft Campbell, Kentucky. The military maintained a rigorous training schedule for the soldiers, and John often wouldn't get home until eight or nine p.m. Exhausted, he would shower, play with Sawyer, and have a little family time before he collapsed into bed. He had to arise by three a.m. each morning to return to the base and would often be gone for days at a time for training.

This grueling schedule went on for weeks, and Sharon and John saw little of each other. They were thankful his training would conclude soon, and they hoped to finally settle into a more normal schedule.

Meanwhile, Sharon had made friends with the women on her street where they lived in Dover, making the best of the lonely hours Often after baking cookies and deserts, she would take Sawyer out in the stroller to visit them and to share her treats. Many of these were widows, who embraced their visits. In a short amount of time, Sharon had developed a circle of friends who'd become a family to help her through her lonely days.

On one particular day, Sharon had worked particularly hard to prepare a special celebration dinner. She set the table with her good crystal, china, and silver and prepared candles for a romantic dinner for two. She could barely contain her excitement as she waited for John to walk through the door and to share her news—she was pregnant again.

That weekend, I'd flown to Louisiana to be the speaker for a Friday night and Saturday conference, and I was also scheduled to speak at two different churches on Sunday during the morning and evening services. After the conference ended on Saturday evening, I prepared for bed around ten p.m. when I received a call from Sharon.

"Momma, I can't find John," she panted frantically into the phone. "He's not home yet, and I know he left the base over an hour ago. I called some of his friends, and they confirmed he left the base. He should be home by now. I don't have a car, so I can't go looking for him. I'm afraid something has happened. What should I do?"

"Maybe he had a flat tire and had to walk back to the base to get help," I suggested, longing to be there to put my arms around her and comfort her. "It would be a long walk. Give him time to do that."

She kept calling the base, talking with John's friends to see if they'd heard anything from him. They knew he left the base, but that's all she could find out. After another hour had passed and still no word, I had to agree with Sharon. Something must have happened.

"Sharon, I phoned Dad and told him you're concerned about John. He's on the way to you."

Acie had a three-hour drive from Memphis to Dover and would arrive at Sharon's home sometime around one a.m.

"Okay, Mom, thanks. I love you. Please pray."

"Honey, just know Dad's coming. Please have him call me when he arrives. I love you too."

We disconnected and I continued to pray.

Sharon called one of the new friends she'd made living on her street who, in turn, called others. In spite of the lateness of the hour, these elderly ladies got out of bed, dressed, and went over to Sharon's house to wait with her until her Daddy arrived.

When Acie drove up to the house in Dover almost three hours later, he was able to immediately access the situation. Three military cars were parked by her house.

After leaving for home, yet still on the base road, John was killed in a car accident. Dog tired, he'd fallen asleep at the wheel, his foot accelerated the car, which hit a tree, and he was killed instantly.

Acie telephoned me in Louisiana to tell me the details. All I could think of was my sweet Sharon and the dreadful pain she was feeling. I couldn't get to her fast enough. I canceled both of my remaining engagements at daybreak and caught the first early morning flight back to Memphis. Acie had taken Sharon and baby Sawyer, now one year old, back to our home in Memphis that night, and I arrived home early the next morning.

Little could comfort Sharon in the days following John's death. His funeral was held at our church in Memphis. She never had the chance to tell him he was to be a father again. She was inconsolable.

A few days later, I drove Sharon to their home in Kentucky and helped her pack up the necessary things and clean out the refrigerator. She stayed with us while trying to work through her grief.

Over the next few months as her belly grew, Sharon took comfort in the fact that John would live on through the lives of his two children—Sawyer and their yet unborn child. Those days were a stark reminder of the verse in James where it says, "Yet you do not know what your life will be like tomorrow. You are *just* a vapor that appears for a little while and then vanishes away" (James 4:14).

Sharon didn't cope well and became suicidal. We were able to get her the help she needed, but her recovery took time. I found myself crying every time I was alone as I watched her struggle.

I once heard someone make the statement, "God doesn't give us the strength to carry someone else's burden, only strength for our own." I understood the meaning of that statement, but when it was my own child who was hurting, my heart was breaking for her. God says there is "a time to weep and a time to laugh" (Ecclesiastes 3:4). We mourn when those we love are hurting. That's not a sign of weakness; Jesus cried when his friend Lazareth was dead because of he loved him.

My digestive system had become paralyzed only five weeks earlier, and it looked like there was no hope for my long-term survival. Though I tried to keep up the speaking engagements, Satan attempted to take my life. The devil used this time to torment me. The thought of my death brought me to the pits of despair as I considered how awful it would be for Sharon and Acie to have to endure double loss. I knew I would be happy in the arms of Jesus, but life on earth would go on for them. This concerned me deeply.

I couldn't allow myself to think that way, but the thought stared me in the face day after day. I knew those thoughts weren't from God. To continue down that path would give Satan an open door in my life. I hadn't yet learned how to take authority over the devil.

Two and three days each week, I had high-stress medical procedures done, and the test results weren't coming back good. I was still in the process of working through things in my own mind and heart and hadn't found the peace that passes all understanding in the midst of my own crisis yet.

My heart broke for Sharon, a pregnant widow, and baby Sawyer without a daddy. I had to be strong and help my daughter adjust to her new life and help her through the unimaginable pain

Sharon and Sawyer needed me, and I needed to be there for them as well as for Acie. We needed each other. Acie was also concerned over my medical issues. He too was feeling I would die. Together, we were all going through deep trials.

Physically and emotionally weak and not too strong spiritually at that moment, I had to ask myself again whether I believed God would heal me a second time. And if it was my time to die, did I believe God was big enough to take care of Acie, Sharon, and little Sawyer? It's not always easy to reach out with strong arms and find God's grace sufficient when in the midst of tragedy. But His grace is always sufficient and enough to meet our every need. He was there for us and we felt His presence near.

I had to take negative thoughts captive and cast them down. We're responsible to reach out and put action behind our faith. I may never have all the answers of why things happened the way they did and when they did. Only God knew that. One thing I knew for sure, God was real, and I could trust him with everything.

30

PLEASE GOD, NOT ANOTHER TRAGEDY?

Eight months had passed since John's death. I could hardly believe Sharon's second baby was almost due. She had one more visit to the doctor prior to the delivery. Everything had been routine up to that point. As she lay on the examining table, the nurse rotated the wand back and forth over Sharon's belly during the final ultrasound to make sure the baby was in position. Immediately, a problem presented itself. The nurse couldn't find a heartbeat. The unexpected had happened. Sharon's baby girl had died in the womb.

The doctor later told us the umbilical cord had twisted around her neck. We were stunned. She named the baby Amanda Ruth Roberts, and once again we were thrust into a time of mourning. To bury her husband and her baby six months apart—to go through such pain and loss seemed more than any human should bear.

The funeral was beyond solemn. We were devastated. Amanda's small body was buried on top of her daddy in the same grave. Who would have thought that John would meet their little girl first? Our hearts were breaking for our daughter. How would she handle this double tragedy? How would we, except with God's help?

Some say tragedies and catastrophe come in sets of three. I'm not superstitious and have never held to such thoughts. But five months later, death came knocking on our door again. Acie's father, Sharon's beloved granddaddy, Acie Willard Ford, whom we all loved dearly, died unexpectedly.

Mother had left the house to get her hair done when she heard this thunderous lightning crash so strongly, she immediately turned her car around to go back to check on Daddy Ford. She found him on the floor by the window between the bed and the wall. We think he'd been looking out at the storm. They said he died of a heart attack when the lightning hit, but no one knows for sure. We attended our third funeral in eleven months.

Grief upon grief doesn't keep time from rolling on. Bills still had to be paid, and my body weakened by the day. The elasticity of my colon gave way from constant use of enemas for two years, and my body could no longer eliminate the water. Dr. Abell prescribed a medication called Colyte. It's a foul-tasting liquid used only in preparation to clean out the system prior to surgery. Considered "Draino for humans," Dr. Abell had never prescribed it to anyone on a weekly basis ever before, but they had no other option for me.

Colyte was an industrial-strength laxative I had to mix with a gallon of water and drink the entire mixture within a three-hour time span. In the beginning, it took effect after drinking the first three glasses or so. Every third day was reserved solely for purifying my system, so I had to cut back my speaking engagements drastically. I wasn't happy about it, but this Colyte procedure zapped me of almost all my strength and energy, leaving me frail and weak. Whenever I was able to fulfill my obligation to speak at a meeting, I had to sit on a tall stool while telling my story.

GOD SAID YES!

I did a lot of deep soul searching over the months that followed as my body strength continued its downward spiral. I determined that rather than praying in defeat or with the same prayer over and over, I would begin to praise God that he was my healer and my deliverer—even in the midst of great sorrow and suffering. The Israelites set the example before us when they marched around the city of Jericho singing praise to God. When they shouted out in praise, the walls of the city collapsed. The Israelites won their battle, and I was determined to win mine.

I remembered how years ago in my youth pastor's basement I was reminded of Paul and Silas who sang praises to God while hanging in stocks in the darkest, dungiest prison cell. They too faced a death sentence. Still, they worshiped God despite their dreadful circumstance, and God responded by sending an earthquake to shake that prison to the core. I chose to praise God in my blindness that night at my youth pastor's home, and freedom came.

Now, I chose praise again. The more my body shut down, the more desperate I became—desperate for God. Affliction often does that. Pain can either drive us away from God or draw us closer to him. The choice is ours. David wrote in Psalm 119:71, "It is good for me that I was afflicted, That I may learn Your statutes." All too aware of my weaknesses, I knew I couldn't do anything without him, including dying.

As a result, I stayed focused on living with a conscious awareness of God's presence in everything. I wanted no separation between my daily life and prayer life. Every second of every day I clung in desperate dependence upon God—the only way I could survive. And because he was my Father and I was his daughter, I wouldn't allow the enemy to heap guilt upon me when I failed.

Yes, I stumbled a lot … even fell down into the deep pit of depression a time or two but never for long. I kept confessing my faith in God, getting back up, and pressing on by sheer faith in his promises. When I was weak, I could feel my Father's arms of grace embracing me. God, in essence, was now my white cane. My physical eyes could see, but now I was blinded by sorrow and suffering of a different kind. Keeping my eyes fixed on him, I could make it through this difficult season with his light leading the pathway, enabling me to take one step at a time.

31

YOU ARE DYING

Dr. Abell felt uneasy about prescribing the Colyte medication. Since they'd never had another patient use it on a regular basis, he didn't know what it might do to my system.

He arranged for me to see a doctor at the Mayo Clinic in Rochester, Minnesota. For the second time in my life, I would go with high hopes that the leading clinic in the world could fix me. I knew Jesus was with me. He had promised, "*I WILL NEVER DESERT YOU, NOR WILL I EVER FORSAKE YOU*" (Hebrews 13:5). Jesus didn't forsake me in my blindness, and he wouldn't forsake me now.

Acie wanted to go to the Mayo Clinic with me, but I was used to having medical testing done weekly and air flights to me were no different than going for another test in Memphis by car. It didn't bother me to make the trip alone, especially since we couldn't afford the additional flight cost. I was confident this would be no different.

Upon arriving at the clinic, I registered at the front desk and was handed my schedule for the week. Testing began almost immediately. Each day, I underwent two to three different types of tests with instruction on what the procedures would involve, with the exception of one particular test.

On the eighth day of medical testing, the doctor told me to catch a shuttle van the next morning from the clinic to go to the St Mary's hospital for the next procedure. I was to arrive by five-thirty a.m.

Shortly after my arrival, a nurse called my name, and she took me to a changing room. The nurse asked me to undress and place my personal items in a locker.

"What kind of a test is this?" I asked.

She expressed deep concern that I hadn't been briefed on the complicated procedure and what to expect.

Oh my, what am I in for? Something told me it wouldn't be easy.

"Time is of the essence," she urged. "We need to get started with this procedure immediately. I'll be with you at all times and will explain it to you as we move through it. Be prepared. It's an all-day test that'll take until nearly nine p.m. when you need to be out front to catch the last shuttle leaving tonight for your ride back to the Clinic."

After the nurse asked me to get on the bed, she left and returned in a few minutes with a bundle of slender tubing draped over her arm. She mentioned that the tube had fine wires inside and would later be connected to a machine. The tube hung down past her hips and resembled layers of garden hose but thinner like a straw. She explained this was to be inserted into my throat and would make its way down through my intestines.

The nurse used numbing spray on my throat, but only one time and just enough to get the procedure started. Then she inserted the tube down my throat. She asked me to keep swallowing as she inched it down further.

She had problems getting the tube through my body. The trap door to my stomach, which she said normally should open automatically every few seconds, wouldn't open.

Another nurse pushed on my abdomen, hoping the pressure might force my stomach door to open enough to get the tube started downward into my stomach. They worked hard and long. Finally, they caught the door slightly open and pushed into it. I had to swallow it inch by inch as she continued moving the tubing downward, which took two hours to complete. The tube's wires extending from my mouth were then attached to a recording device at the foot of my bed. I must have looked like something right out of a science fiction horror movie, with tubing protruding from my mouth connected to an eerie machine.

Around noon, the nurse came to my bedside with a boiled potato, a small chicken breast and one-fourth of a cup of liquid. I was to eat it within twenty minutes with this tubing in my throat. Her instructions were very specific, "Go easy on the liquid. This fourth cup is all you can have. Anything less than total compliance means we have to do the test all over again at another time."

Never am I going through this again! I tried to eat the dry chicken breast with the tubing and wires in my mouth, and with difficulty, I got it down within the time limit.

From morning until late evening, I lay there as my body attempted to digest the meal, and the machine scratched lines reacting to every move in my digestive system.

Later that evening, a different nurse disconnected me from the machine. Then she began extracting the tubing from my throat hand-over-hand as fast as she could. This caused me to choke. I threw my hands into the air, pleading for her to stop. If she continued in that manner, it would damage my throat.

"Oh, does it hurt?" she commented after noticing my distress. "I'm sorry."

"Please pull slowly," I wrote on the notepad.

She agreed and asked if I was ready to start again. I was, but it still wasn't easy. I choked and gagged with every pull.

Meanwhile, she kept saying, "Stay calm, stay calm; take it easy."

Finally, the last of the tubing came out, and I was free. But one challenge quickly turned into another.

"It's nine-forty p.m. You'll need to get dressed quickly and get to the front door of the hospital as fast as you can to catch the ten p.m. shuttle back to the main clinic and from there to your motel. This is the last shuttle of the day, and you don't want to miss it. If you do, you'll need to call a taxi."

Wow, fifteen minutes to dress, follow the hallways, and get out of there?

By now, the stress of the day had taken its toll. Almost as soon as I got on the shuttle, I started having sharp pains in my neck, left arm, and chest. Thinking the testing had been too much for me, I wondered if it could be signs of a heart attack.

As soon as I got back to my hotel room, I called Acie. He wanted me to get checked out, but the hour was late, and the clinic had closed for the night. After lying in bed talking with him for a while, the pain eased up. It had been a highly strenuous day, and I was simply dead tired.

The next morning, I was scheduled for more tests at the clinic at eight a.m. The pain had subsided, so I mustered up a positive attitude and felt like the tests would be easier. Nothing could be as difficult as this day had been. And with that in mind, I fell asleep. The following day I pressed forward with the remaining tests.

After ten days of testing, the physician assigned to my case discussed all the test results with me. I desperately desired good news. He compassionately explained that my stomach, intestines, and colon were totally paralyzed. There was no movement of muscles contracting, not even four inches anywhere. Therefore, typical procedures such as ileostomy, colostomy, G-tube, J-tube, or stomach pacemaker wouldn't work in my case. He also confirmed that a surgical bypass wouldn't be possible either because my pelvic floor muscles were paralyzed. No surgery or procedure available to modern medicine would help me.

The doctor advised me to continue using the Colyte mixture for as long as possible. "It won't work indefinitely," he explained. "But use it as long as you can. I don't know what effects it'll have on the rest of your body. It may work for a couple weeks, two months, or maybe a little longer. We don't know. We've never given this to a patient on an ongoing basis and don't know how long before the elasticity of the colon will give way to it like the enemas and become ineffective. When Colyte stops working, we have no other options. There's nothing we can do. Your life will be short-lived. Go home and get your house in order."

Where had I heard those words before? *You're blind, Marolyn. There's nothing we can do. No surgery or glasses will help. Go home and learn to live with it.*

With that, he handed me a prescription for Colyte. I took hold of it as my heart sunk low. He had given me absolutely no hope. Once again, I needed a miracle.

I now gave God my full attention. If he could heal my eyes, he certainly could heal my paralyzed digestive system. Only this time, if my miracle didn't come, instead of needing a white cane, I would need a casket.

❧

Doctors suggested surgery to remove my nonworking colon and intestines. I declined because I believed God for a miracle and wanted to keep everything in place as long as no danger existed. The doctor confirmed there was no danger in declining the surgery. So, Acie and I would leave the rest up to God.

For the next six months, I continued to use the gallon of Colyte to force my body to eliminate waste and toxins. I dreaded days when I'd have to drink the nasty mixture and suffer that incredible pain.

In time, the elasticity of my colon weakened. My body began holding the gallon of liquid from early morning to well into the night before it would expel, causing excruciating pain. Nothing gave me relief. Facing the worst physical suffering I'd ever endured, I often thought I'd actually die during the process. But what choice did I have? I had to keep taking the medicine.

32

MINISTRY HELPED ME NOT TO GIVE UP

God opened doors for me to share my story from Johannesburg down to the tip of South Africa, all over England, Paris, Ireland, Switzerland, and Spain during the earlier years of my digestive failure. Keeping busy actually helped me to endure my illness. Having to study and prepare my spirit for my conference teaching sessions and sharing my blind eyes miracle story strengthened me every time I bragged on what Jesus had done for me—a constant reminder to keep believing the promises of God. I needed that. The location, whether at home or abroad, made no difference, I scheduled my speaking engagements on the days I wasn't taking the Colyte medication.

Some people couldn't understand my drive to keep my speaking engagements alive. That determination kept my faith alive. Sharing my miracle story helped strengthen my own faith to believe God for another miracle. Also, I knew if I ever completely stopped and gave in to my illness, I would become a total burden on Acie.

His heart was breaking over my illness, and he knew the pain I suffered. He was tender, loving, and compassionate through all the years I was sick. Little did I know back on the farm in Michigan that those characteristics which I prayed for in the guy I would someday marry would be the exact characteristics I would desperately need most in the years to come. Acie was always there to hold me in his arms and help me find some sense of security with what was happening to me. I couldn't have endured it without him and my Lord.

The day came when I no longer accepted speaking engagements overseas. The elasticity of the colon had all but totally become impervious to the Colyte medication, so I was fighting to live. Whatever it took to keep my dependence and trust in the Lord alive and strong within my own spirit, that's what I did.

The pain was so intense I had to keep moving in order to bear it. To take the medicine every third day was always pure torture. I'd go back and forth between sitting, lying, standing, and rolling in order to handle the pain and get my body to flush itself.

After I used the enemas for two years, the elasticity of the colon had become resistant to the enemas so in a matter of time, the Colyte would become ineffective as well. My life had become dreadful, but it was life, nonetheless. Thankful to be alive and able to minister and serve my Lord. my testimony became powerful, and people were coming to Jesus as a result.

One example was a man named Roy Brunson. I met Roy when he sat down next to me on an airplane headed for the Memphis Airport. Roy had been a vice-president of a Fortune 500 company, a multi-millionaire, and a hardcore atheist. From childhood, his mother had drilled into him that a God who allowed evil in the world couldn't possibly exist, and Jesus wasn't real.

Then one day, Roy's world came crashing down. After a series of sour business deals, he found himself broke, devastated, angry, and seriously contemplating suicide upon his arrival home.

With hatred he asked, "If you think Jesus is real, tell me; what has he ever done for you?"

"Do you want me to tell you?" I asked.

He nodded.

I then shared how I had been blind for thirteen years, and Jesus give sight to my blind eyes. Roy didn't commit suicide. Instead, he found out Jesus was real and accepted him as his Lord and Savior. He wound up starting a new company/organization, World Light Ministries, and became an evangelist and missionary to the Ukraine and Africa. At last count, before his death a couple years ago, Roy had led nearly 250,000 people to faith in Christ along with starting numerous orphanages.

What happened to change Roy's mind and life? He credits sitting next to someone on that airplane as the one single event in his life being the catalyst to his salvation and rebirth. Roy says in his own words, "After Marolyn Ford told me her story, I realized it could only be a miracle. Her blue eyes looked right through me into my soul. I was very frightened. Could my mother be wrong? Was there really a God who loved me and had a plan for my life?"

Stories like these are why I continued to push myself as hard as I did.

Not all were large crowds either. I'd speak wherever I was asked to go. Once I was honored to speak at an underground gathering. This special group meeting was held in a warehouse. As we entered through metal doors, I had to let my eyes adjust to the dimly lit area before venturing further in. As I scanned the interior, I noticed the dirty cement floor—and the doors and windows were protected with security bars and heavy locks.

Before the man lowered the barred door down, he looked to make sure no one was out there. Only thirteen people were present, but that didn't matter. This was an opportunity to share how the power of God had set me free from blindness and to present the Gospel. Eight out of the thirteen people accepted Jesus Christ as their Savior,

Someone once said, "Circumstances merely provide you with the opportunity to reveal the extent of your faith in the promises of God." My circumstances in life were a real test as I continued with my ministry. At times, I felt I couldn't keep going, but I held on to the promise "I can do all things through Him who strengthens me" (Philippians 4:13).

As far as my illness was concerned, no one could do anything to help me, so I didn't want to make a big deal about it. I was keenly aware that unless a miracle occurred, things would eventually digress and shut me down. So, I pushed for as long as I could.

Unfortunately, the medical challenges I faced began to rapidly deplete my energy. My strength had diminished to the extent that my neurologist prescribed an electric power scooter to enable me to get around. She said the thin membrane like the one between the eggshell and the egg or covering a chicken breast had disappeared and caused my muscle weakness. I was grateful for the independence this afforded me and was able to continue with my speaking engagements but on a more limited basis.

Eventually, I became confined to the power chair for all activities. Normal actions such as washing dishes, doing laundry, and cooking were now major challenges. I'd become too weak to carry a plate of food or a small pan of water.

I used the power chair for everything. It became my work tool as well as my transportation. On laundry day, I pulled the clothes basket behind me as I made my way from the bedroom to the laundry room. I could at least accomplish some of the regular duties around the house.

But as my condition deteriorated, the day came when I could no longer continue even the simplest household tasks. The burden fell on Acie to perform the everyday jobs around the house after working a full day in the ministry.

Then one day, the Colyte medication couldn't pass through my body. My temperature rose, and I thought I would die during the procedure. I'd been on it for two years. As predicted, my colon had lost all its elasticity.

At a loss to know how to proceed, Dr. Abell suggested that I take an enema along with drinking the Colyte medication. However, my body couldn't handle that. It caused excessive vomiting

I hit bottom and was left with the impression from the Mayo Clinic specialist nothing more could be done. I honestly thought I had medically come to the end of the rope. Except for a miracle, death was now at my door.

Two questions continued to weigh heavily on my mind. First, would God give me a second miracle of equal magnitude as the healing of my blind eyes?

The devil tormented me, saying, "You can't expect that. Who are you that you should obtain another miracle?"

The second question was whether I had faith to continue standing on the Word and believing for a second miracle of equal magnitude as the first.

These same questions hit me again and again. Over the years, I read every book I could find on prayer, trust, faith, and hope in order to stir up my faith, to find the strength to take hold of God's Word, to stand on his prayer promises, and to receive answers.

One of the first things I learned from reading what others wrote about prayer was I must not separate the spirit of my daily life from the spirit of my prayer time. I was to take the Holy

Spirit with me everywhere I went and include him consciously in everything I did and not leave him behind when I say, "Amen." That wasn't easy to do. It took concentration and a deliberate act of my will to abide in that close fellowship with God.

I found it difficult to hold strong in my faith while waiting on God for healing. Moment by moment I made the effort to keep my mind disciplined by "taking every thought captive" (II Corinthians l0:5). Often, I felt overwhelmed with despair, but I had to keep God's Word always before my eyes and in my heart while focusing my "eyes on Jesus, the author and perfecter of faith" (Hebrews 12:2).

At this point, I realized that when my mind was weak, God saw my heart. When I failed to maintain this discipline, I felt disappointed with myself before God. Yet, God doesn't want me to be down on myself but to simply confess that I left God the Holy Spirit behind, get back up, and go on walking in victory rather than defeat.

God knew my heart and knew his Word was my delight. David said, "If Your law had not been my delight, Then I would have perished in my affliction. I will never forget Your precepts, For by them You have revived me" (Psalm 119:92-93). This verse carried a lot of weight for me as I faced a need so great only God could answer, yet at times it seemed he didn't. I actively sought the answers to these questions.

Jesus teaches us to "Have faith in God" (Mark 11:22)—the Living God. Like someone has said, "Let faith focus on God more than the thing promised, because it is his love, his power, his living presence that will awaken and work faith." These words encouraged me to continue pressing in.

To endure long-term, chronic, life-threatening hardship required strength beyond myself. Yet God promised, "My grace is sufficient for you, for power is perfected in weakness" (II

Corinthians 12:9). He gave me his strength—not before it was needed but on an as-needed basis.

What would I have done if I hadn't had faith in God and in what he could do? At least I had hope. I talked with him about my daily concerns—the pain, my daily activities, my joys and discouragements. Through everything I endured, he cared about what concerned me. He wanted to be my friend.

In those darkest hours, I found strength with God's supernatural power undergirding me. The question became then, how could I trust God when all hope was gone? I had to learn to run to God as my place of refuge and safety. "He who dwells in the shelter of the Most High will abide in the shadow of the Almighty" (Psalm 91:1).

Only there in God's presence did I feel secure.

33

BEDFAST

Four years had passed since the accident in our Jacuzzi. In so many ways, the fact that my body had survived as long as it had was a miracle. As the doctors predicted, the elasticity of the colon had given way completely to the Colyte treatment. My esophagus had also been affected. I could no longer get food or liquid down and had become a mere skeleton, weighing under ninety-four pounds. My tongue was glued to the roof of my mouth by morning, and my lips stuck to my teeth. I had to work it loose every morning and upon awakening during the long nights.

"Marolyn, we have to get you to the hospital," Acie insisted one day after noticing my lips. He knew something was amiss.

At the emergency room, one of the attending nurses took one look at me and took charge. "Lay down here—you're dehydrated. We'll get the IV going as quickly as possible."

Dr. Abell came in and immediately admitted me for acute malnutrition and dehydration. My body was no longer able to survive without outside help. "Marolyn," he said, "we'll need to proceed to nutritional feeding immediately so you can get the nutrition you need."

A Hickman catheter was inserted through my chest into my subclavian heart vein and Total Parenteral Nutrition Feeding (TPN) was administered through IV. This nutritional feeding

(TPN) would make the difference between life and death for me, at least for a while.

I expected the inevitable would come quickly, but to my surprise, Dr. Abell placed me on long-term nutritional feeding to give me extended life. I didn't know he'd do that when many other doctors wouldn't have, except on a short-term basis. Dr. Abell was able to place me on it for a longer time because he was a research doctor, and I became his "human research monkey," so to speak.

I was thankful for God's protection and watchful care over me. At the time, I didn't realize this would be an on-going treatment. I thought it would be a temporary fix. He literally saved my life over the long run—truly a God-thing, even though I didn't recognize it at the time.

The computer pump nearly drove me batty those first few nights of being attached to the nutritional feeding. This procedure was my life-support, and my existence depended upon it. But for me, the sound of the machine was scary—like someone gasping for breath every few seconds. That itself gave me overwhelming anxiety. I was unable to sleep from thinking about all that was happening. Often, in the middle of the night, I stared at the shadows on the ceiling and walls coming in through the windows. Tormenting thoughts ran through my mind—terrifying feelings of finality, loss, confusion, despair, and hopelessness.

I didn't know how long Dr. Abell would keep me on TPN feeding or how long I could live on it. He'd informed me that even though I was on Nutritional Feeding, man can only make certain ingredients, and when the body depletes itself of those ingredients only God can make, I would die.

Because of the serious nature of the procedure, the doctors had to keep checking my blood and adjusting my nutritional feeding intake to get it balanced according to my bodily requirements. Soon, I was told I'd be able to go home on this program, but before I could be released, they had to train me on how to become my own nurse and manage the feeding tube and meds.

A nurse was assigned to teach me in three one-hour sessions on how to use the TPN computerized pump and the IV equipment, and how to insert the vitamins, liquids, and protein into the nutritional feeding IV bags. They taught me what size of needles and syringes to use to draw out the different amounts of medications. Different sized needles were necessary for different medications, and I had to remember to use the saline and heparin before and after each injection. There were a lot of do's and don'ts on how to bandage the IV site.

I remained in the hospital for twenty-one long days. As badly as I wanted to go home, though, I was terrified of being on my own and leaving the security of the hospital. Thankfully, a homecare nurse would help me get set up and check on me regularly. I was discharged from the hospital around ten-thirty that night.

I knew my condition was serious when a hospital bed was delivered to our house close to midnight. They moved our bed over, and suddenly, our bedroom was transformed into a hospital room. Thank goodness we had a large bedroom. The entire ordeal was unexpected and overwhelming. I simply hadn't given any forethought as to what my going home would require. I had no idea they would bring in the bed and all the three-foot-square boxes filled with medical supplies.

But that wasn't all. A refrigerator was also delivered in which to place the nutritional feeding bags of liquid. I was so glad we had space in the laundry room for it. Those bags couldn't be placed in our kitchen fridge, and nothing but those bags were to be placed in this medical refrigerator. The bags could get contaminated. The home care nurse arrived that night around one a.m. and had to scramble through the boxes of medical supplies to locate all the many items needed to reconnect me to the nutritional feeding bag which had been removed from me before I left the hospital.

The next day Acie purchased three white cabinets on wheels for easy moving to the bedside several times a day. Each cabinet contained four draws. The medical supplies and the cabinets where the supplies were stored had to be kept completely sanitary.

In the days that followed, whenever the nurse wasn't there, my hands shook from weakness as I worked through the process of adding ingredients to the bag of nutrition and while working with the needles and syringes to medicate myself. All the while, I was plagued with questions.

What if I measure out and inject too much medication by mistake? What if the feeding line becomes contaminated? What if I don't see the air in the tubing and it goes to my heart? What if I step on my tubing while getting out of bed or it catches on something and breaks off at the site in my chest? What if the tubing pulls out of my chest at night when I turn over in the bed? My thoughts were embedded with fear. This "what if" business wasn't like me.

A little blanket fuzz or dust floating in the air getting between any one of the twenty-five- to-thirty needles and syringes used to administer medications inserted through the Hickman line port could contaminate the line and cause a blood infection. The responsibility of keeping it all sanitary and free of contamination was a must. Still, sepsis infections were inevitable.

The complications of long-term TPN nutritional feeding were severe blood infections, liver failure, and bone deterioration, but I couldn't live without it. I'd have to be connected to it eighteen hours daily for the rest of my life. Though everything about it was frightening, I was thankful to have it.

I had to turn my what-ifs over to Jesus—the One who is faithful. Each day I had to make the conscious choice to entrust my life to his faithfulness. If I could trust him with my eternal soul and the pardon of my sins, why was I struggling to trust him with this?

Boxes of hospital paraphernalia with the numerous tubes, catheters, bandages, syringes, leg bags, and medications needed to keep me alive filled the room.

During those first months, I was emotionally weak and fragile. On numerous occasions, I wept in Acie's arms, unable to cope. In addition to all we'd been through in the past few years—my son-in-law's tragic death, my grandchild's death, Sharon's pain, Acie's father dying, and my own body betraying me—I was also feeling the loss of having to cancel all my speaking engagements.

Now, with my health failing further, I was bedfast for months and didn't know if I would ever again return to ministry. Even so, I still felt God had a plan for my life. Throughout my whole ordeal, I never felt as if God abandoned me. Yes, I didn't understand why God was allowing this to happen, but desertion on his part never entered my mind.

Right then and there, I made the decision to storm the gates of hell full throttle in spiritual warfare. The enemy would not win this battle. When the doctors couldn't cure the sickness, God could. I had to win this battle the same way others had—by overcoming Satan because of "the blood of the Lamb and because of the word of their testimony" (Revelation 12:11) through taking hold of those things that were rightfully mine which were bought for me with the precious blood of Jesus and by the power of his resurrection.

"Bless the Lord, O my soul," David penned. "And forget none of His benefits, Who pardons all your iniquities, Who heals all your diseases" (Psalm 103:2-3). I had to embrace *all* his benefits, and that included my healing. God meant what he said, or he wouldn't have said it. I had a solid foundation upon which I could stand on my faith. As long as I held on to God's promise and looked to Jesus as my healer, my faith wouldn't waiver.

Looking back through the years of sharing my miracle testimony about my blind eyes that could see, my faith was strengthened. I now faced an immediate need for another healing, and I'm glad I kept sharing in meetings or my faith might have weakened over time.

34

HUNGER PAINS, PIZZA CRUST, & DEATH

The day eventually came when I once again was strong enough to be able to go out to keep my doctor appointments but upon returning home, I had to go right back to bed.

The two most urgent needs of the human body are for water and food. I hadn't been able to drink anything or digest food for months. One would think my body would've learned by then that no substance was coming. Even so, I continually wrestled with hunger pains and unquenchable cravings unable to be satisfied.

When I was able to be up for short moments of time in my power chair, I'd head to the refrigerator and pantry and gaze longingly at the food, praying that one day I might be able to eat again. In an odd way, I gained an element of satisfaction in that activity. It helped me deal with my hunger.

When I asked my doctor if there was anything I could do about the terrible hunger pains, he told me, "As long as you live, the hunger sensation will never stop. The nerves responsible for the hunger sensation are still working, sending alarm signals that you're hungry and thirsty to the brain. The fact that you can't eat or try to ignore these alarms doesn't kill the nerves. Eating is a vital part of normal bodily function. It's like the man without legs who still feels his toes."

One day, I'd strongly desire a certain kind of food; the next day a different food. Even though I couldn't eat, smelling what my body craved gave me some type of satisfaction as well as extreme frustration.

I missed the feeling of a full tummy or a cup of hot tea going down and warming my body, especially on cold days.

For lack of use, the muscles in my jaw became so tight, it hurt to yawn. When I spoke with my physician regarding this tightness, he prescribed a simple treatment. "You need to chew on something tough; you're getting lockjaw," he said. "Jaw muscles need to be exercised just like any other muscle."

Chewing on the outer edge of a pizza crust worked best for exercising my jaw. Unlike bread that crumbles, the tough pizza crust held together. I could chew on it like a doggy bone and spit it out.

When someone asked me about not being able to eat, often their reaction was, "Oh well, at least you can taste and spit out. That's not so bad. Things could be worse."

Well, all I can say is it's not as easy as it sounds, and it really didn't work. Being unable to eat is horrible. In years gone by, I thought being blind was the worst thing that could happen to me, but not being able to eat and satisfy my hunger and thirst was actually more devastating. To chew and spit out only brought about manifold frustrations. I struggled with this inability to eat every hour of every day for eight years. My entire body screamed out for food and became a nonstop battle, but I had to be satisfied with the intravenous feedings.

The Hickman line inserted through my chest and into my subclavian heart vein had two ports that hung down at my waist. One port was used to administer the TPN which dripped eighteen hours daily. The other port was used to administer my medications. These ports became infected frequently and would set off sepsis infections in my blood. A serious sepsis infection quickly became a matter of life and death because it went right into the blood stream and heart. These infections became more recurrent as time progressed and my body weakened.

This turned out to be a twelve-year illness. I was on the TPN for eight years. In the early years of taking the TPN feedings, the infections came about once a year, then twice yearly, then every four months, and then every three weeks. I was in and out of the hospital constantly, never knowing whether I'd survive another infection.

STAT was written across my medical records. If I started a half degree of fever, I was to make a fast beeline to the emergency room. When the nurses saw STAT on my medical records, they knew this was a life and death situation, and I was taken in immediately. As the years progressed and my body weakened still further, these infections came upon me as frequently as every three weeks. When they did, I'd be hospitalized, followed by a recuperation period at home with homecare nurses because I was bedfast. The infections also became more difficult to get under control while hospitalized, and my recovery time in bed lengthened. Each time, my body further weakened. It slowly was depleting itself of the natural nutrients that only God could make within the human body.

All this made me think much about my death, which isn't necessarily a morbid thing. We should think more about death. David wrote, "So teach us to number our days, That we may present to You a heart of wisdom" (Psalm 90:12).

Author John Ryle wrote in his book *Practical Religion*:

> Sickness helps remind men of death. The most live as if they were never going to die. They follow business, or pleasure, or politics or science as if earth was their eternal home.

They plan and scheme for the future, like the rich fool in
the parable, as if they had a long lease on life, and were not
tenants at will. A heavy illness sometimes goes far to dispel
these delusions. It awakens men from their day-dreams and
reminds them that they have to die as well as live. Now this
I say emphatically is a mighty good.[1]

"It is appointed for men to die once and after this comes
judgment" (Hebrews 9:27-28), meaning we face God Almighty
himself.

Even though my faith wavered at times, and I can't say I
never doubted God, he knew my heart. A powerful force within
my spirit enabled me to take possession of what God said was
mine—healing. It's in the blood covenant. In faith, I expected
to receive God's blessings. That's essential to answered prayers.

Often during those years, the pain became too much for me
to bear. Even when it seemed as if death was knocking at my
door, I continued to trust God as I ran the race set before me.
My days were numbered, and my life was in God's hands.

I had learned down through the years that knowing the Lord
and walking in fellowship with him, I could depend on him to
direct my steps, and when the trials and tragedies come—and
they did—God was with me. He never left me nor forsook his
child. God is real. After all, he'd instantaneously healed my eyes,
but would he heal me a second time? He certainly could.

Live or die, I was at peace.

35

SAYING GOODBYE

I never stopped praying and believing that one day I'd be able to eat again, even though the doctors declared it medically impossible. My paralyzed digestive system had atrophied. Day after day I didn't see any change for the better. I cried out to God, "Lord, it was thirteen years before you opened my blind eyes to see. Please don't let it be thirteen years before you touch and heal my body so I can eat again."

I became so weak I couldn't turn the house doorknobs. Blood reports showed my blood nutrient levels had dropped far too low. This caused me to develop intractable mouth ulcers. My regular doctor was out of town and the fill-in physician treated each ulcer with silver nitrate. Instead of healing the ulcers, they multiplied. The next day, more than sixty ulcers covered the inside of my mouth, tongue, soft palate, and throat. I couldn't bear for my tongue to touch my teeth or make contact with the ulcers. The suffering became unimaginable. I felt like Job who had sores break out all over his body.

Later that evening, Acie thought I was asleep in my wheelchair. He tried to awaken me to move me to the bed. When I didn't awaken, he realized something was wrong. He immediately called my home care nurse and told her the situation. She called in paramedics who stabilized me and whisked me away to the hospital.

Acie learned that I hadn't been asleep. Rather, I was in something like a coma. Over the course of the next three weeks, I lingered between this world and the next. Meanwhile, the ulcers kept multiplying.

The doctor told Acie the ulcers were probably also in my stomach. During the following days, whenever the medication wore off before the appointed time when I could take more, I awoke in excruciating pain. Acie tried comforting me and loving me through it. He never left my side while the unbearable pain continued for three weeks. I was stuck in that state and showed no sign of improvement.

The doctor looked Acie straight in the eyes. "I don't see any way your wife will pull through this," she said. "You need to prepare for her death."

Crushed to the core, he left the hospital to make the arrangements for my funeral.

Thirteen days passed, and instead of dying, I surprised the doctor and nurses by fully regaining consciousness. Now the doctor told Acie he needed to prepare for me to enter a nursing home. So, he made the necessary preparations.

However, about a week later, I was allowed to return home with a homecare nurse. Acie gathered me into his arms, grateful for whatever time he had left with me.

That first night, Acie dreamed we were in heaven together. When he awoke, he told me, "Marolyn, in my dream you had been completely healed. There were no nutritional feeding tubes, urinal catheters, alcohol pads, or medications. Your personality was very outgoing, cheerful and entertaining. You were telling everyone what great things God had done for you."

But what did that mean? Was I going to die and receive my new heavenly body, and then Acie would later join me? Neither of us knew how to interpret the dream. I drifted through the following weeks in weakness and in pain.

During the months ahead, I was in and out of the hospital with sepsis infections. Sepsis occurs when chemicals released into the blood to fight the infection start an inflammatory reaction throughout the body. A little dust or blanket fuzz floating in the air, coming between one of the twenty-five to thirty needles used daily to medicate myself while on the Nutritional Feeding would set up Sepsis infections in my blood, which went right to my heart. This inflammation triggers a cascade of changes that can damage multiple organ systems and cause them to fail.

Confined to bed, I often fought for my life due to sepsis infections.

John, our daughter Sharon's second husband came to me when I'd been totally bedfast, and it didn't look like I would live long. He asked me how I'd feel if he said they wanted to make a move to Alaska. As much as the thought of it hurt me deeply, and realizing that if I died, Acie would be alone in his grief, I didn't know how to answer him. To me, the timing was bad. We loved them dearly, and it would be hard to see them make a move like that.

John had two children, Brittany and Johnny, and Sharon had little Sawyer from her first marriage and another new baby on the way. I needed them so desperately at that time, and I thought I'd never ever see them again—or the new baby. But I knew he had to live his life in the best interest of his family.

But after more conversation on the matter, I said I wouldn't want to stand in the way of him fulfilling his boyhood dream. Sharon also had often, through the years, spoken of her desire to live in deep-snow country one day. They both had the same desire since their childhood days—a dream come true for both of them. What else could I say?

Acie voiced his feelings to a friend, "Sharon and the kids are leaving for Alaska, and Marolyn is going to heaven soon." The reality of the impending transition hit him hard. His heart was wrenched.

Meanwhile, I became weaker. When I spoke, my voice to trembled and created a heavy feeling in my chest.

Someone actually asked me, "Marolyn, don't you ever feel like curling up in a ball and just lying there until you die?"

"To be honest," I replied, "sometimes, yes."

My physical body was exhausted, and I could've easily given up, but the Holy Spirit inside me wouldn't let me. I'd come to the point where something had to give.

36

ANGELS OF MERCY

After developing another bout with sepsis, I ended up right back in the hospital needing constant care once again. When dismissed from the hospital, Acie took over working alongside my homecare nurses. Our mornings began earlier than usual so Acie would have time to tend to my needs. First, he placed a thick towel beside me on the bed in preparation for brushing my teeth, changed me into a fresh gown, and combed my hair as best he could. He helped me with the nutritional feeding, syringes, needles, and medications and tended to the bedside bag before thee home care-nurse came in. Then he left for work.

When he came home from work, he bathed me and actually washed my hair in the bed as needed. I knew I looked bad, but Acie always told me I was beautiful to him. Many husbands or wives leave their partners when chronic illness strikes but not Acie. I'll be eternally grateful for his unconditional love and support. Only through genuine commitment to the marriage vows could someone stay with a spouse through difficult, long drawn-out months and years.

And Acie walked through the journey not just once but twice—first through thirteen years of blindness and now, this twelve-year bout with digestive failure illness. He often said, "Marolyn, everything I do for you is a joy because you make it easy for me." His was an example of the true bond of marriage, love, and sacrifice.

I can't say enough about the love my husband showed toward me and that of my "angels of mercy." I want to name them because they deserve to be honored, but I won't for fear I might leave out a name. Even though I had the homecare nurses coming in daily—these whom I called my angels—other angels too numerous to name also showed God's love by their willingness to give of their time and energy to go the extra mile to help us. This was the first time we received this kind of attention and we greatly appreciated it.

One day a church member asked if she could clean my house on a weekly basis. I couldn't believe I heard that correctly. I never expected such a blessing. She was the first to make such a sacrifice. When it became too much for her, she asked three others to come alongside to help her clean.

Later, Acie needed someone to sit with me during another long recovery following hospitalization with pneumonia and sepsis infection crisis for about four weeks so he could be freed up to do his ministry work on the church field. A lady picked up on his request for help and set up a temporary network of ladies who took turns staying with me and tending to my care during the days that followed. While there, they assisted with household duties like folding clothes left in the dryer. This woman also arranged to have different people bring in evening meals for Acie—only enough for one person—delivered in throw away containers. Another lady volunteered to tailor my clothes to fit as I dropped from a size eight to a junior three slim. One sweet friend telephoned me every day for twelve years to encourage me, while another brought fresh flowers she picked out of her garden weekly.

And another friend offered the simple gift of a ride in the car. One day she simply stated, "When you get strong enough, I'm going to take you for a ride in my car just to give you a change of scenery. You don't even have to dress to go out. Just a housecoat will do. You let me know when and if you feel like you could do that." She made the offer week after week with a tender heart.

Months had passed. Finally, the time came when I was able to take her up on her offer. After my strength improved some, she volunteered to drive me to all my doctor and therapy appointments weekly over the next eight years, with the exceptions when Acie felt he needed to go with me to talk with the doctor. It freed him up so he could faithfully fulfill his ministerial responsibilities. And she loved doing that for me. It kept her busy. She loved doing this for us and told me her life was more fulfilling and meaningful to be able to do this for me.

In order to restore muscle tone, my neurologist prescribed water aerobics therapy three times weekly. This lady who drove me to all my appointments assisted me in and out of the pool and into my wheelchair, which was extremely difficult for me as well as for her. My muscles had atrophied significantly from the many months I'd been bedfast. While in the pool, I enjoyed getting to know and connecting with others suffering from loss of body functions. Their friendships bathed me in comfort.

After assisting me out of the pool, my precious angel would push me back to the locker room where she also helped me shower and dress. Again, not an easy task. Between showering and dressing, she had to change the medical bandage covering the area where my IV tubing extended from my chest. I'd always been very modest and embarrassed for anyone other than Acie to see my naked body. That all had to change as I was unable to do these things for myself now. My life now became about survival rather than my sense of modesty. This girl had a great sense of humor, which made it easier for me to accept and feel comfortable with her assistance.

This was truly an example of the Church acting as Jesus's hands and feet—a practical application of love poured out on both Acie and me.

Medical bills continued to mount. My chronic illness caused financial disaster within the household. My medical bills came to over $300,000 annually. The paperwork we had to file with the hospital and insurance company was daunting. Even in this area, God provided us the help of an incredible woman who was a business manager for a group of doctors. She understood medical insurance papers and invoices and asked if we would trust her enough to handle this for us. What a stress reliever. We didn't have to sort through all the paperwork and billing statements. She was even able to get some of the blood work bills written off for us—a tremendous answer to prayer.

Each of these women shared a part of their lives using their God-given gifts during this season of chronic illness. They truly acted as Jesus's hands reaching out to us.

Later, I was admitted into the hospital again and needed a blood transfusion. Within hours, my twin sister, Carolyn, hopped on a flight to Memphis for the transfusion. Doctors didn't know if I would pull through. I was so sick, speaking out of my mind, hallucinating, and unconscious for days. I'm so grateful to her and the many other close friends who were willing to get involved, go the second mile, and do what they could to help during this challenging time.

When Carolyn had to return home, another friend who came by the hospital to pay me a visit decided to stay with me. She sat by my bedside day and night until the crisis was over.

On several hospitalizations, friends stayed with me night and day so Acie could get some sleep and be faithful with his work responsibilities. One of these ladies who came to see me in the hospital with her husband took my panties and gowns home and washed them and returned them the following day.

These hospital crisis times happened time and time again. There's no way I could write about all of them or individually thank each person who came to our rescue and helped me. I prayed that God will bless them for their unselfish willingness to help in innumerable ways.

The mounting medical costs became a big concern for us. Because of my long-term illness, my medical bills were staggering. Thankfully, we had good insurance coverage, but would it last? Fortunately for us, God sent another angel of mercy to address this.

I'd been admitted into the hospital at the time this telephone call came through. A lady from our medical insurance company asked which doctors I'd seen during the past three months. She then inquired further as to what tests they ran. She concluded the call by asking which doctors I was scheduled to meet with during the next three months and the tests the doctors might want to schedule me for. I had no idea.

I thought the call strange but didn't think about it any further until three months later when I received another call from this same lady and was asked the same questions. This time, however, her questions made me feel uncomfortable. Maybe the insurance company was going to make trouble for us because my medical care was so costly.

Then a few months later in mid-October, she telephoned again.

This time, however, as we engaged further in discussion, I realized she was actually trying to protect us from financial disaster. She called to let us know we'd soon be approaching the $1 million cap on our insurance policy, and if I had to be hospitalized one more time that year we would cap out and have no coverage. We hadn't been aware we were so close to the cap. She explained that in order to have financial protection, we could make a switch to a policy coverage that didn't have a cap, but we'd have to make the switch immediately.

We'll forever be grateful to this lady and the insurance company for bringing this matter to our attention and for guiding us through it. I often regretted not getting her name but have often thought of the blessing she was to us by giving attention to my insurance coverage. I would love to have the opportunity to thank her personally.

She switched us to a policy without a cap that year. Unfortunately, this switch also meant I'd no longer be under the care of the University of Tennessee medical research physicians who knew and understood my case studies. I'd been with the UT physicians for eight years from the beginning of my illness. This was the hardest part of the policy changeover but unfortunately was unavoidable if we wished to maintain insurance coverage.

After much prayer, we selected the doctors who we felt to be the best primary care physician, gastroenterologist, urologist, neurologist, and blood specialist we could locate to take over my care. We decided to meet these new doctors before the new policy would go into effect on January 1st. I needed to know they had my medical records and knowledge of my condition in case of an emergency such as entering the hospital unconscious and not being unable to explain my medical problems and needs to them.

We met with each of these new doctors the week of Christmas. Good thing too. One week later, the new insurance coverage and new medical team took over. I became critically ill and admitted to the hospital on January 2nd. God had directed our steps in the nick of time. Again, I was in very serious condition with another septic attack.

Hundreds of get well cards and letters poured in from France, Switzerland, South Africa, Spain, Ireland, Scotland, India, England, and from our precious homefront friends. A genuine outpouring of concern and affection came our way and encouraged me in ways I can't begin to relay. Friends in Florida had received word that Marolyn Ford had died, so we received bereavement cards as well. That was sweet.

In reality, it all boiled down to the one thing Jesus taught as the *golden rule*. "Treat others the same way you want them to treat you "(Luke 6:31). There is true power in our acts of kindness.

37

A WORD FROM GOD

Once home again, I needed a homecare nurse daily. Weakened in body and mind, unable to formulate a prayer or bring to mind memorized Scriptures, I went down in despair.

One day, I was paging though an old hymn book and came across the song "Leave It There," written by C. Albert Tindley. In great feebleness and with tears streaming down my face, I read the second verse, "If your body suffers pain … and your health you can't regain; and your soul is sinking in despair." Those words hit me; that's right where I was. My mind and soul were in despair, my body in pain, and my health I couldn't regain.

The song went on, "Jesus knows the pain you feel. He can save and he can heal." When I read that, I knew I would be healed.

Suddenly, I experienced a deep, inner witness in my spirit and a confidence to continue to believe I would be healed. I received only what I can describe as a gift of faith. I simply knew I was going to be healed. God had spoken it.

The song ends with, "Take your burden to the Lord and leave it there." I burst into tears and rejoiced in God, my Jehovah Rapha, my healer. With hope restored and with joy and excitement in his promise to touch and heal my body, I said with tear filled eyes, "Thank you! Thank you, Jesus." I needed the words to this song. I read them repeatedly as a prayer to the Lord, and it strengthened me.

On the outside, though, nothing had changed. I hadn't eaten anything in eight years. Man can't reproduce exactly the nutrients God makes, and those nutrients had left my body. I was still a dying woman. Yet, in my heart something had shifted. It wasn't a matter of *if* but a matter of *when* I would be healed. Waiting on God's timing was very difficult, but I had a Word from him! And a Word from God makes all the difference.

But in the natural, things looked bleak. My body was no longer able to fight the blood infections, and I contracted double pneumonia with fluid building up in my lungs, a urinary tract infection, and an infected Hickman line. For eleven days, I dropped in and out of consciousness. Death again came knocking as my body temperature soared.

Finally, the doctors were able to get my body temperature to return to a more normal range, and I was released from the hospital so I could recuperate at home with my homecare nurse.

A few days after having been dismissed from the hospital, my home healthcare nurse was convinced something was wrong. He immediately got in touch with my primary care physician who called for an ambulance to pick me up from my home and take me to her office.

The attendants rolled me in through the back door on the gurney. The doctor drew blood and did some medical tests before she had the ambulance driver take me back home to wait for the results.

As they rolled me out the door, the doctor said, "Just as soon as I receive the test results, I'll call you."

A couple hours later, she called, saying, "Get someone to pack your bags for the hospital. An ambulance is on the way to your house as we are speaking. I arranged for you to have a heart test before they give you a room. We need to know whether or not the infection has reached your heart, and there's no time to waste. It's a matter of life and death if the infection reaches your heart. When you get to the hospital, you'll bypass the emergency room and go immediately for the heart tests. The hospital technician is expecting you and is putting everything on hold for your arrival. The ambulance is already on its way."

It was touch and go for a few days, but God miraculously pulled me through it yet again. The crisis was over.

Again, I was released from the hospital with home nursing care. This was my third hospital stay within six weeks. But I had to believe God would be faithful to the Word he spoke into my spirit that day.

38

Tell Him "I Am"

The ingredients in my body that only God could make, man couldn't completely replicate in the nutritional feeding. These had left my body, and that was why I became skin and bones. The doctor had told me that when my body depleted itself of those ingredients that only God can make, I would die from the lack of those nutrients. I also couldn't lose any more weight. That day was fast coming upon me. I weighed ninety-four pounds—the lowest I could go and still live.

I'd barely been awake over the last few weeks, except during my medication time. I knew I was dying. And this particular moment in the dark of night, I wondered if I'd even make it to morning. We held on to God's promise of healing for twelve long years.

Acie told his best friend, Reverend Kenny Bruce, "I never know when I come home or wake up if she'll be with me or if I might find her dead and gone to heaven."

I didn't fear dying and being with the Lord; that would be awesome. But in my heart, I wanted to live lor   feel my life's purpose and destiny were yet fulfilled.
to do on earth.

At one o'clock in the morning, I was so w
reach over to wake Acie. I could hardly sp

without needing to pause for air. Tears coursed down my cheeks as I spoke.

"Acie, we … need … to … pray … one … last time." In my own way, I was saying goodbye. I didn't want him to wake up and find me gone to heaven without closure.

Acie immediately jumped up, wide awake. Worn-out and disillusioned, he tried to prepare himself for my death, though he didn't want to let me go. He had little left to give. Acie had taken care of me through thirteen years of blindness and twelve years of digestive failure. He knew the inevitable was coming. He'd emotionally struggled in agony and anguish twenty-four hours a day over my pending death. His heart was breaking. Yet, he still had a childlike faith God wanted all of us to have. God was our only hope.

Mustering up what little faith he could, he whispered, "Lord, you can touch and heal Marolyn. You can do it. In Jesus's Name, Amen." That was it. But prayer can be like that sometimes. In reality, we were driving a stake into eternity. We were on God's timing. Due to my near vegetable state, I closed my eyes and immediately fell back to sleep.

When morning dawned, I could hardly believe I was still alive. And on earth. Not only that, but my body wasn't trembling on the inside like it had been during the night. I felt better … noticeably better. Could it be God healed my digestive system last night when we prayed? When God restored sight to my blind eyes, I knew instantly I'd been healed because I could see. But it would take longer to know whether my digestive system was working again.

Even so, I was alive and still on earth—cause for great rejoicing. I instantly recalled earlier when God had spoken to through the song "Leave It There," reminding me that he saves and heals. Maybe this was God's time for me. Could it be? Had he healed me? I was still extremely weak in body.

Acie had left for work before I woke up that morning. He had to be at the hospital very early to pray for someone before the man went in for surgery and to be there for the wife and family. My homecare nurse was somewhere in the house, but I was alone in the bedroom.

My nurse came into my room as was our routine. Once a week, she would drop a blueberry into my mouth to stimulate my taste buds so I wouldn't lose my ability to taste. To my surprise, this time as I swished it around to touch the taste buds in the back of my mouth, it actually went down!

Although too weak to outwardly rejoice, my spirit shouted on the inside.

I hadn't been able to swallow anything in eight long years. Nothing! I always tried, but my digestive system was completely paralyzed. Eating and digestion had been impossible. The Mayo Clinic and all the other doctors said I would never eat again.

But I really ate something!

Glory! Glory! Hallelujah! Thank you, Jesus!

The nurse phoned Acie for me and held the receiver to my ear and mouth. I struggled for air and had to take a breath between syllables but finally got the words out. "Acie, I ... can ... eat. A blue ... berry ... went ... down!"

The nurse drew the phone back to herself, so I didn't hear his response as he talked further with her. After she hung up, she called my GI doctor to report my progress and tell him I swallowed a blueberry.

"That's not possible," he said.

Overhearing their conversation, I responded in my weakness, "Tell him ... I did."

I think he heard me in spite of my weak voice. The nurse insisted on what she'd seen, and he finally instructed her I was *not* to eat any more food. Instead, I was to start drinking Ensure, a highly caloric liquid food supplement.

"Let's see how she does with that. Call me back when she can drink one-fourth of a bottle."

On his way home from work, Acie purchased the bottles of Ensure.

Meanwhile, Acie had phoned journalist David Waters, a writer for the mid-south and metro Memphis *Commercial Appeal* newspaper, who'd been writing a series of articles about my illness to keep the community informed about my progress—since I was a local author—and shared the news about my miracle. He wrote how Marolyn Ford swallowed a blueberry and was now on Ensure liquid drink.

Wow! What a turn of events. What a testimony of God's power to heal.

David wrote an article to document my miraculous healing. The Howard Scripps wire service picked up the story, and the news of the miracle spread.

In four weeks, I was able to drink one full bottle of Ensure. Still bedfast and also on the IV nutritional feeding, my strength gradually returned to me over time. God truly had done a miracle.

One month later, although I was still extremely weak, Acie wanted to take me to the mall. I thought it was for a change of pace. Hurriedly pushing me in my wheelchair, he passed all the stores he normally shopped at, and I wondered where he might be going in such a hurry.

All of a sudden he stopped, leaned over my shoulder and asked, "Would you like to go into the cafeteria here for a bite to eat? It's our anniversary."

"Oh, wow!" I said, "It is? Our anniversary?"

Christmas, birthday, and anniversary celebrations were something in my past. They came and went and didn't register with me. I'd been too ill to think on those things. I still couldn't eat much yet, but that wasn't the point. I hadn't eaten in a restaurant in years. I was as excited as a little kid anticipating a new toy. I'd dreamed of the day when I would be able to eat again. I was so happy we could celebrate our anniversary together that day. I could eat!

The prayer I had prayed so often over the years, "Lord, it was thirteen years before you opened my blind eyes to see. Please don't let it be thirteen years before you touch and my heal body so I can eat again" was answered. It had been a twelve-year waiting process, but I never gave up. Our God, the God who created the universe, saw, heard and answered my prayer. There was, is, and never will be any other God like him.

Acie wheeled me over to a table and then went through the cafeteria line to pick out the food for us. It wasn't much, but I ate one soft green bean, a nibble of fish, and a sip of soup from Acie's bowl. That was a lot for me. Acie couldn't take his eyes off me. He was as excited as I was. This was an anniversary celebration I'd never forget.

Although it had been approximately four weeks since the miracle when I started on the Ensure drink and my digestive tract started working, my doctor kept me on the nutritional feeding a little longer. I got another blood infection in my Hickman line and had to return to the hospital. I'd been drinking the Ensure since July 21st.

While in the hospital this time, the nurse told me David's article was posted on the mirror in the doctor's lounge so everyone could read about my healing. I was surprised someone put that there in the hospital for all to see. But it stood as a testimony to show God's healing power in today's world.

The doctor removed the infected catheter from my chest. When the infection in my blood was under control, he looked at me and said, "Keep drinking the Ensure, and start eating three small meals daily. The Ensure will help bring up your blood levels and strength." With a smile on his face he continued, "You're doing wonderful, keep up the good work. Come back in three months, and if you don't need me, cancel your appointment. But you can call me anytime."

He gave me a hug and walked out the door to see his next patient. I didn't need to see him again. My last trip to the hospital, where they were very familiar with my case, had been evidence to the medical community that God had indeed healed me.

I can't begin to describe the freedom I felt that day as I was completely disconnected from the IV feeding tube once and for all. I could go home without it. Like a bird let out of the cage, I'd been set free. My healing was now complete. I left the hospital and never looked back. The battle had been won.

"The Lord sets the prisoners free. The Lord opens the eyes of the blind; The Lord raises up those who are bowed down; The Lord loves the righteous (Psalm 146:7-8)."

"How blessed is he whose help is the God of Jacob, Whose hope is in the LORD his God, who made heaven and earth, the sea and all that is in them (Psalm 146:5-6)."

The truth of David Waters's article couldn't be clearer. "Here is a blind woman who sees. A woman who could not eat or drink yet lives." The truth of it filled me to overflowing.

GOD SAID YES!

What a great and mighty God I serve! He delivered me out of the worst of it to bring me to his highest best. Now I could share his goodness across the nations and impart lasting hope. God didn't just heal me once but twice.

Like a songbird released from its imprisoning cage, God had given me a reason to sing my heart out. To sing with rekindled faith and joy. What he had done for me, he could do for others. God said, "Yes," revealing his faithfulness again and again. I would see it with my eyes and be able to celebrate it standing tall, sure, and whole.

39

LIFE GOES ON

A massive heart attack took Acie's life unexpectedly on September 20, 2014. My beloved husband is now in heaven where there will be no time factor involved in our being apart. For him, it will be as though he left me less than five minutes ago. However, I was left to continue alone down here, and it took months to readjust to a life without my special partner with whom I shared my trials and experiences of joy. I never felt so alone.

He stuck by my side when most people these days would've turned and run. He was a strong man of God who influenced a lot of people. If I would've had a chance to kiss and hug him goodbye before he died, the adjustment would've been much easier. I still long for one last hug.

Only God can fill that lonely gap in my life. I lean upon Jesus when needing friendship or comfort and to feel I'm loved during the long, lonely hours. I can reach up and tell Jesus, "I need a hug." He's there all the time. He never leaves me, and he hears my deepest heart cry. He satisfies my every longing as I open myself up to acknowledge his nearness.

Life goes on. I've begun to adjust as I draw upon the pieces of life's puzzle with God's hand upon me, guiding me onward. I draw strength from activities I'm now free to investigate.

After the miracle, even though I could eat anything my heart desired with no limitations, my body still remained weak. It has taken years to regain those nutrients I couldn't get from the man-made nutritional feeding. So sometimes, I'm seen using a power chair, but less often now that time has progressed, and my body has strengthened.

Healthy and well, I'm currently in the midst of writing another book and am planning an extended mission trip involving speaking in crusades and conference meetings in three foreign countries before returning back to the USA. Also, I have more TV and radio interviews coming up. God showed me I would be going abroad to minister to the nations. The doors opened without my seeking them out.

I plan to live life to the fullest, praising God for his wonderful mercy and grace. Sharing my miracles is a vehicle to show God's power and glory until Christ returns.

ABOUT THE AUTHOR

Marolyn Ford is a well-known inspirational speaker and singer and has spoken to hundreds of thousands of people worldwide to groups as large as thirty thousand and climbing. Her story, after experiencing two documented miracles of life-changing proportions, reveals God's power and desire to heal today just as in times past.

Marolyn's story is about God's authentic *miracles* in the literal sense of the word. They are well-documented by the medical community and are available to any who would ask for a copy.

She has shared the stage with well-known men and women of God such as Rev. James Robison, Dr. Jack Graham, Lindsey Roberts, Dr. Adrian Rogers, Dr. Bailey Smith, Governor Huckabee and many others. She was interviewed by several National TV Hosts including Dr. Pat Robertson, Rev. Rev. Paul Crouch, Rev. Rev.James Robison, Rev. Jim Bakker, Sheila Walsh, Rev. Gordon Robertson, Terry Meeuwsen, and Ben Kinchlow and many others. Several movies and documentaries have been written and produced based on Marolyn's life.

She is the author of three books including, *These Blind Eyes Now See, Walking and Talking with Jesus,* and *Grace to Endure,* and two CD's in which she inspires and challenges her audience to new levels of faith. Marolyn has received numerous awards over forty-seven years of ministry and continues to inspire audiences with her tenacious faith as she travels internationally. Marolyn received her Doctorate from Primus Universtiy, Phoenix, Arizona.

If this book has ministered to you or if you have committed to become a follower of Jesus, Marolyn would love to hear from you. Please email her at: marolynford@bellsouth.net.

She is available to inspire and challenge audiences wherever God opens the door, so don't hesitate to contact her to schedule a speaking engagement. Go to marolynford.com for more information.

ENDNOTES

1. Ryle, John Charles, *Practical Religion*, (Baker Book House, Grand Rapids, MI. © 1977.) page 360.

Made in the USA
Columbia, SC
11 July 2020